Successful Retirement

Copyright ©1998, 1996
The Kiplinger Washington Editors, Inc.
All rights reserved

No part of this book may be reproduced or transmitted in any form or by any means, electronic or mechanical, including photocopying, recording or by an information storage and retrieval system, without the written permission of the Publisher, except where permitted by law.

Executive Producers:
Thomas L. Conrad
Conrad & Associates, Inc.

Frank B. Phillippi
The Kiplinger Washington Editors, Inc.

Cover and text designed by S. Laird Jenkins Corp.

ISBN: 0-938721-48-8

Manufactured in the United States of America

Second Edition: April 1998

Successful Retirement is available in bulk quantities at discounts.

For more information, contact:
  Conrad and Associates, Inc.
  10415 Stapleford Hall Drive
  Potomac, Maryland 20854
  301–983–6417
  800–553–0504

This package has been designed as an educational tool. While providing information, it is not intended to provide advice for specific individuals and should not be relied upon as the basis for investment or legal decisions. The authors and producers disclaim all responsibility for misunderstandings and specific positions taken by the viewers and readers of this product.

Acknowledgments

Kiplinger has been helping people plan for their retirement for many years in many forums. *Kiplinger's Personal Finance Magazine* offers ideas and reports on retirement trends on a regular basis. *Kiplinger's Retirement Report* presents monthly guidance on all aspects of retirement, both for those already retired and for people approaching it. Kiplinger Books publishes two guides: *12 Steps to a Worry-Free Retirement* helps readers develop a sound financial plan, and *Retire & Thrive* helps them determine what to do with their time once they retire.

Successful Retirement is the latest manifestation of this advice. Written in plain English, it presents a practical, *achievable* plan for creating the nest egg needed to assure a financially secure retirement. But a truly successful retirement requires more than financial security. This guidebook addresses these other issues as well, including whether or not to work in retirement; how to determine where you'll live; ways to enjoy your leisure time; and how to protect your nest egg with adequate health insurance and a sensible estate plan.

Many people contributed their knowledge to ensure the information contained in this video and guidebook meet Kiplinger's highest standards.

The guidebook was written by Susan Phillips, managing editor of *Kiplinger's Retirement Report,* and edited by David Harrison. Kim Walker Klarman checked the manuscript for accuracy; Dianne Olsufka proofread it, and Karmela Lejarde offered editorial assistance.

Thanks, also, to Frank Phillippi and to the staff at Alan Weiss Productions for their contributions to the video and to the families and individuals who shared their experiences and insights with our viewers.

Contents

Introduction 1

Part 1: Where the Money Will Come From 3
1. Your Pension 4
    Making the Most of Your Defined-contribution Plan
    Understanding a Defined-benefit Pension
    What It Means to Be Vested
    Dealing with Multiple Pensions
    How Safe Is Your Plan?
2. What to Expect from Social Security 15
    Who Can Collect?
    Estimating Your Benefit
    Understanding Benefits for Couples
    How Your Benefits Will Be Taxed
    The Late Retirement Bonus
    Continuing to Work while You Collect
3. Saving on Your Own 24
    Individual Retirement Accounts
    Keoghs and SEPs for the Self-employed
    Choosing an Annuity

Part 2: Taking Stock of Where You Are 35
4. What You'll Need 36
    Tracking Your Spending
    Estimating Your Retirement Income Needs
    Factoring in Post-retirement Inflation
5. What You'll Have 42
    Totaling Up Your Income and Assets
    Determining Your Income Gap
6. Closing the Gap 45
    Comparing Your Nest Egg with Your Needs
    Boosting Your Savings
    Adjusting Your Goals
7. Is Early Retirement an Option? 51
    The Impact on Your Pension
    Sizing Up a Golden Handshake

Part 3: Making Your Money Work for You **55**
8. Creating an Investment Strategy **56**
    Investment Options: Stocks, Bonds, Mutual Funds and Real Estate
    Allocating Your Assets
    Using a Financial Adviser
9. Planning Your Pension Payout **72**
    Annuity Options
    IRA Rollovers
    Lump-sum payouts
    Making Your Choice
10. Tapping the Money in Your Home **79**
    Tax Advantages of Selling Your Home
    Pros and Cons of Reverse Mortgages
    Using a Sale-Leaseback

Part 4: Making Lifestyle Decisions **85**
11. Working in Retirement **86**
    Finding Your Second Career
    Starting Your Own Business
    Going Back to School
12. Where Will You Live? **96**
    Resources That Can Help
    Choosing Your New Home
    Considering a Retirement Community
13. Enjoying Your Leisure **106**
    Volunteering Your Time and Skills
    Starting a New Hobby

Part 5: Protecting Your Assets **111**
14. A Health Care Safety Net **113**
    Your Employer's Plan
    Understanding Medicare
    Choosing Medigap Coverage
15. Do You Need Long-Term-Care Insurance? **119**
    What Medicare Covers
    Who Needs Insurance?
    Choosing a Policy
16. A Plan for Your Estate **125**
    Assessing Your Need for Life Insurance
    A Well-crafted Will
    Other Important Pieces of Your Plan

Conclusion **133**

Introduction

A s with many of life's milestones—your first job, getting married, buying a home, having children—retirement stirs up a mixture of excitement and fear. There's anticipation for the long-awaited freedom from the daily grind—a chance to do what you want with your time, whether it be traveling, spending more time with family and friends, turning your hobby into a small business or getting involved in local government or a charitable cause.

But retirement is also clouded with uncertainty. Are you saving enough to sustain the kind of lifestyle you want and still make your money last? Do you and your spouse have adequate and secure health coverage, and the means to provide the daily care one or both of you may need as you age?

A 1995 survey by Keyport Life Insurance Company showed that 43% percent of those surveyed said they didn't know how much they needed to save for retirement and only 46% thought they would meet their financial goals for retirement.

Instead of letting such concerns and uncertainty darken your retirement outlook, start planning for your retirement today. *Successful Retirement* can help you confront your concerns realistically and start taking steps toward achieving your goals.

No matter how far you are from retirement, it's not too early to start planning and making decisions. If you haven't yet decided when you want to retire, do it now. This decision doesn't have to be set in stone, but it helps to have a goal in mind. The more specific you can be about how much money you'll need and when you'll need it, the more likely you are to be able to do what it takes to meet those goals.

Part 1

Where the Money Will Come From

The crucial first step in planning for retirement is estimating how much income you will have when you retire. For most people, retirement income comes from three main sources: a pension of some sort, social security and their own savings and investments. How well you understand and make use of each of these income sources is likely to have a significant impact on the quality of your retirement. So before you start setting goals for your retirement and determining what kind of lifestyle you'll want to maintain, let's first examine these three sources so you'll know how to use them to your best advantage.

Chapter 1

Your Pension

You probably expect the bulk of your retirement income to come from your pension. But surprisingly, recent data from the Social Security Administration shows that among 65+ households only 18% of income comes from pensions or annuities. The rest breaks down like this: 42% from Social Security, 18% from employment, 18% from assets and 4% from other sources. That highlights the fact that many people will have to continue working after they retire (see page 86) and underscores the importance of saving on your own for retirement, which we discuss in Chapter 3. However, for some—particularly people in the upper income-tax brackets—pensions will continue to be an important source of income.

If you stay with the same company for most of your career and your employer offers a generous pension benefit based on salary and years of service, you can probably expect to have a significant amount of your retirement income needs covered by your pension. But for more and more people, that's just not the case. Increasingly, employers are shifting from traditional pension plans, where the employer foots the bill and directs the investing, to defined-contribution plans, such as 401(k)s, that require you to set aside some of your paycheck to fund your retirement, usually with the employer matching at least part of your contribution. Or you may have hopped around from job to job before settling down, leaving you with a number of small pensions.

For these reasons and more, it's important that you understand your pension situation and determine how to make it work as hard for you as you worked for it.

Making the Most of Your Defined-contribution Plan

Defined-contribution plans don't promise you a specific pension benefit when you retire as traditional plans do. Instead, the company contributes and/or allows you to contribute money every year to a fund for your retirement. The amount is usually a percentage of your salary or it may be based on profits; it can be fixed or fluctuate from year to year. Plans vary quite a bit: Some allow you to contribute 4% or 5% of your salary each year, but contributions limits can range from as little as 2% to as much as 15%.

The money contributed to your account grows untaxed until you tap it in retirement. If the investments do well, you end up with more at retirement. But if they don't, your benefit will suffer. You bear the risk.

The most well-known type of defined-contribution plan is the 401(k), which is named for the section of the tax code that created it. But 403(b)s—the 401(k)'s nonprofit cousin—profit-sharing plans and Employee Stock-Ownership Plans, or ESOPs, are also defined-contribution plans.

401(k) Plans

These allow you to contribute up to several thousand dollars a year from your salary to a retirement fund. The maximum allowed by law in 1998 is $10,000. (The dollar maximum is adjusted for inflation each year and then rounded down to the nearest $500 increment.) Your personal limit depends on your salary and your plan's rules; most firms allow contributions of between 2% and 15% of pay.

You decide how the money will be invested, choosing from options that usually includes a half dozen or so stock and bond mutual funds and guaranteed investment contracts (GICs), which offer a set interest rate for a specific period of time. But increasingly employers are offering larger pools of mutual funds, including funds from different fund companies.

Some plans are even offering employees the right to invest their 401(k) money in individual stocks and bonds. If you are intimidated by the task of choosing among your plan's options, ask your plan administrator for more guidance. Also, consult the explanation of different types of investments that begins on page 56. In general, if you're ten or more years from retirement, you should have 60% to 80% of your 401(k) money invested in stock funds or individual stocks.

401(k)s offer employees a one-two tax-savings punch: Salary diverted to the plan doesn't show up as taxable income, which gives you the same result as if you reported the income and then got to deduct the contribution. And interest, dividends and capital gains earned inside the plan aren't taxed until withdrawn.

In addition, many 401(k)s offer an added bonus to participants: The employer will match part of your annual contribution to the plan. For every dollar you contribute, your employer may kick in another 25 cents, 50 cents or even a dollar, up to an established limit. That's free money—a guaranteed return on your investment. As of 1995, 90% of plans offered some sort of match—that's up from 78% in 1994—according to a survey of large defined-contribution plans (averaging 5,500 participants) by Rogers Casey and the Institute of Management and Administration. If you have a plan with a generous employer match, that's even more reason to contribute as much as you can possibly afford.

Keep in mind that some restrictions come along with the tax incentives. Since the idea is to encourage saving for retirement, you generally can't get your money out of the plan until you leave the company, unless you die or become disabled first. If you do leave the company before age 59½ and want to take the money with you, you can avoid all penalties and withholding by having your employer transfer the money *directly* to an IRA or your new employer's plan. If you take the money yourself, you'll have 60 days to roll it into an IRA or your new employer's plan, but you'll be hit with a 20% withholding bill from the IRS. (If you roll the money over within 60 days, you'll get that 20% back, but only when you file your next tax return; meantime the money's not working for you.) If you decide to hold on to the money longer than 60 days, you'll be hit with an early-withdrawal penalty (not recuperable) in addition to the 20% withholding.

As with most IRS rules, there are exceptions. For example, you're allowed penalty-free withdrawals at any age if you withdraw the money in roughly equal installments at a rate that should deplete the account over your lifetime, but the withdrawals will be taxed in your top bracket. The withdrawals must continue for at least five consecutive years *and* until you're 59½. Also, 401(k) plans can permit their participants to *borrow* from their accounts. However, there are restrictions on this, and plans are not required to allow it.

403(b) Plans

These plans are similar to 401(k)s, but are offered to employees of schools, hospitals and other nonprofit organizations. Overall, the plans work the same: The money going into the plan is subtracted from your pay and not taxed until withdrawal. Also, 403(b)s generally allow participants to contribute as much as 20% of gross pay, up to a maximum of $10,000 a year (this will rise in tandem with the 401(k) limit in $500 increments). But maximum contributions can vary from plan to plan so to make sure you don't contribute too much—in which case you may have to withdraw the extra money and pay taxes and a penalty on it—ask your plan administrator about the limit that applies to you.

Most 403(b) plans offer employees a limited number of investment options—usually fixed or variable annuities from insurance companies (more about annuities beginning on page 30). Because of this, 403(b)s are often referred to as "tax-sheltered annuities." But you actually aren't limited to investing in annuities. Although your plan administrator may not tell you this, by law you are permitted to transfer your 403(b) money to a *403(b)(7) custodial account* at a mutual fund company or brokerage firm—giving up the guarantees an annuity offers for a shot at higher returns and probably lower annual fees. You also can't borrow against the money—loans are permitted with 403(b)s, as they are with 401(k)s, but *not* with 403(b)(7)s.

If you would like to move some or all of your money into a custodial account with a wider range of investment choices, begin by contacting the mutual fund, brokerage or bank where you want the money invested. Ask about the procedures for arranging a direct transfer from a 403(b) plan. If your plan administrator is not aware of your right to move your money, refer him or her to IRS Revenue Ruling 90-24. Keep in mind that if you've only recently started contributing to a 403(b) annuity, you're likely to be hit with a surrender charge of as much as 7% for withdrawing money from it. But most annuities have a "free withdrawal" clause that allows you to take out 10% of the balance each year without incurring surrender charges.

Another point for employees of non-profits: Starting in 1997, non-profit organizations—with the exception of state and local governments—are permitted to set up 401(k)s for their employees. It's hard to say how many will do this, but it's something to be on the lookout for.

Profit-sharing Plans

With these plans, your employer makes annual contributions to your retirement fund based on the company's profitability. Some allow you to make additional contributions, some don't. If your company does well over the years, profit sharing can provide you with a nice nest egg. And if the money in the plan is at least partially invested in stocks, this retirement account should outpace inflation over time.

The problem with this type of plan is that because the size of annual contributions will vary and future investment performance is unpredictable, it's difficult to get a handle on how much you're likely to have when you retire. But you can make a rough estimate by asking your benefits department what the average contribution has been over the past ten to 20 years and getting historical information on how the plan's investments have performed.

ESOPs

Employee stock-ownership plans are actually one kind of profit-sharing plan. Instead of contributing money, in these plans the company contributes shares of its stock or allows you to buy shares as an investment option. This way you can accumulate your company's stock while paying little or nothing in commissions, and sometimes at a discount from the market price. Most ESOPs are offered by small private firms, not by large companies with publicly traded stock.

How much you gain from participation in an ESOP depends on your company's future success. For that reason, consider the plan carefully in comparison to the other retirement options your company offers. You won't have all your eggs in one basket if you can also participate in a 401(k) or defined-benefit plan.

Once you reach age 55 and have been in the plan for ten years, you have the option to move up to 25% of your money out of the ESOP and into other investments. At age 60 you can move as much as 50% of the money if you choose. Once you're within 5 years of retirement, it's wise to have no more than 15% to 20% of your total retirement savings invested in your company's stock.

Understanding a Defined-benefit Pension

The more traditional defined-benefit pension plan promises you a specific retirement benefit for life, based on your salary, age and how long you work for the company. To receive the maximum pension, most plans require you to work at the company for 30 years and retire on or after the "full retirement age"—usually 62 or 65. Other plans use a point system: Once your age plus the number of years you worked for the company total a certain number of points, you can retire with full benefits. A typical defined-benefit pension will replace about 37% of income for a worker who stays with a company for 30 years and retires at a salary level of $50,000.

The formula for calculating benefits normally works like this: Each year you're with the company earns you a monthly pension benefit equal to 1.5% of your "final average monthly earnings." Many companies define "final average monthly earnings" as the average of your salary during your last five years on the job. For example, say your company uses a 1.5% accrual rate and you retire at 65 after working there 20 years. Your accrued benefit would be 30% (20 x 0.015). If the average of your salary during your last five years is $66,000 ($5,500 per month), your monthly pension will be $1,650 (0.30 x $5,500). Some firms base final earnings on the average of your last three years on the job, which makes for a more generous pension because the average pay during your last three years is usually higher.

You don't take on any market risk with a defined-benefit plan. The company promises to pay you a specific amount of money based on its formula and then invests money over the years to keep that promise. If the investments come up short, the company is required under law to make up the difference. So the company suffers the consequences of poor investment performance, not you. (See page 13 for a discussion of what happens when the company goes out of business or can't afford to pay.)

The risk you *do* face with a defined-benefit plan is that inflation will eat away at the value of your benefit over the years. A recent study by the General Accounting Office found that the proportion of private pension plans providing cost-of-living adjustments (COLAs) had declined from 54% to 10% in recent years. And only about half of all states provide automatic COLAs to their government retirees. So don't forget to factor in inflation when looking at how much income your defined-benefit pension will provide. Without COLAs, an amount that sounds large at first won't be worth nearly as much as the years wear on. If inflation averages 4% per year, for example, each $1,000 of benefits will have the buying power of only $665 within ten years and $542 after 15 years.

That's why it's important for people with defined-benefit pensions to make sure they have inflation protection built into their other income sources. Social Security benefits, for example, are currently indexed to inflation (see page 18 for more on that). You'll also want to invest your nest egg so that it will earn enough to keep up with inflation and provide the income you'll need. There'll be more discussion of that in Part 2.

What It Means to Be Vested

Before you start estimating the benefits you could accumulate in your company's plan, you need to understand "vesting." Becoming vested in an employer's pension plan means working for the company long enough to acquire a nonforfeitable right to receive a pension. Usually you have to work for an employer for several years before you become fully vested.

Federal law gives companies two basic choices for vesting their employees. One is called "cliff" vesting: You lock in your right to the plan's benefits after five years of service; before that, you're entitled to nothing. The other choice is a gradual or graded vesting schedule, in which you become vested gradually over the years. The law requires that you be at least 20% vested after three years and fully vested after seven. Here's what the two different methods might look like:

| | Percent Vested ||
Years on the job	Cliff Vesting	Gradual Vesting
1	0%	0%
2	0	0
3	0	20
4	0	40
5	100	60
6		80
7		100

With cliff vesting, if you leave before becoming vested, you give up all rights to benefits. But you do get back any money you contributed to the plan, plus the interest or dividends it earned. With gradual vesting, if you leave the job after becoming partially vested, you're entitled to a partial pension at the time of your departure. But it probably won't be worth very much, as we explain in the next section.

In a defined-contribution plan, being fully vested means you can take all the money in your account with you if you leave, but you'll be hit with penalties (see page 6) unless you arrange a direct transfer to an IRA or to your new employer's plan. Money you contribute to the plan yourself is automatically fully vested; you can take it with you when you leave, no matter how long you've been with the company. In a defined-benefit plan, being fully vested means you've earned the right to receive a pension when you retire, but most employers will make you wait until a specified retirement age to start collecting.

There are some exceptions to these basic rules of vesting. For example, at age 65, you are fully vested no matter how briefly you've been on the job. If your employer decides to terminate its pension plan, you also become fully vested automatically. Or, if you're under a union contract or another situation in which more than one company pays into your plan, you may not be eligible for full vesting until you've worked for the company ten years.

Dealing with Multiple Pensions

When it comes to pensions, more is not necessarily better. Even though five- or seven-year vesting allows you to move from company to company and become vested in several plans during your career, a bunch of small pensions usually provides less in total benefits than one full pension. Here's why:
- You earn relatively meager benefits during the early years on the job. Really significant amounts of money don't start to build up until you've been with a plan for 10, 20 or more years.
- Most defined-benefit plans penalize you for leaving the company before normal retirement age, usually 65.

If you are ten to 15 years from retirement and in a defined-benefit plan, you stand to lose a lot by switching jobs. Not only do you lose the peak pension-earning years at your current company, but also you may not be at your new company long enough to earn a full pension. If you plan to leave under those circumstances, negotiate with your prospective employer to try to get compensation for what you're losing in pension benefits.

With defined-contribution plans, less damage is likely to be done by switching jobs. If you are fully vested and leave the company, you're simply entitled to whatever is in your retirement account at the time as long as you arrange a direct transfer into your next employer's plan or into an IRA.

How Safe Is Your Plan?

The good news is that most pension plan participants—either in defined-benefit or defined-contribution plans—needn't be concerned about the safety of their plan. But it's still important to understand your rights as a participant and to know how to recognize warning signs that your plan may be in jeopardy.

Defined-benefit Plans

Most qualified defined-benefit plans at private companies are insured by the Pension Benefit Guaranty Corporation (PBGC), an agency of the federal government. If a plan covered by the PBGC becomes unable to pay benefits or goes out of business, the PBGC will take over payment up to a certain annual limit per person. In 1998, the limit is $34,568 for a person retiring at age 65; the figure is adjusted annually for inflation. Ask your benefits administrator whether your plan carries PBGC protection. If it doesn't, find out why.

The PBGC also keeps track of which defined-benefit plans are underfunded, meaning they haven't set aside enough money to cover the pension benefits they've promised. Any plans less than 90% funded are required to notify their participants. If you receive such a notice, it doesn't necessarily signal disaster, but it should prompt you to find out more about your plan's financial situation.

Defined-contribution Plans

These plans are not insured by the PBGC, but, along with other pensions, they are regulated by the Pension and Welfare Benefits Administration (PWBA). The biggest problems with these plans are management delays in funding employee accounts and diversion of funds for other company uses. These problems tend to occur mostly at small companies and don't seem to be widespread, but the number of troubled plans the PWBA encounters has been growing in recent years. It encourages participants to watchdog their plans, particularly if the company is having financial problems or they notice that contributions are not being credited to their accounts within 90 days.

The bottom line is the more you know about your plan, the more likely you are to notice any signs of trouble. Read plan documents carefully, especially the Summary Plan Description (SPD) and the Summary Annual Report. The SPD is designed to be a plain-English description of the plan and should explain the amount of benefits, requirements for qualifying and anything that might prevent participants from receiving benefits. Pay particular attention to the specific examples of how benefits will be paid.

If you see or hear anything disturbing about your plan, get a copy of the full annual report (Form 5500) from your plan administrator or from the Department of Labor (either way you'll pay copying costs).

For more information about pension safety:
- *Your Pension Guarantee* (stock #068-000-00004-1) is available from the PBGC. Send $1.50 to the Superintendent of Documents, Government Printing Office, P.O. Box 371954, Pittsburgh, PA 15250-7954; or call 202–512–1800.
- *Your 401(k) Plan: Building Toward Your Retirement Security* (stock #D15975) and *Your Pension Plan: A Guide to Getting Through The Maze* (stock #D13533) are free publications from the American Association of Retired Persons. Send your requests to AARP Fulfillment, 601 E St., N.W., Washington, DC 20049.
- For help with pension problems, contact one of the PWBA's field offices. They are located in Atlanta; Boston; Chicago; Dallas; Detroit; Fort Wright, Ky.; Kansas City, Mo.; Los Angeles; Miami, Fl.; New York City; Philadelphia; St. Louis; San Francisco; Seattle; and Washington, D.C.

Chapter 2

What to Expect from Social Security

Despite what you may have heard about the future of social security, it *will* be there for you, in one form or another, when you retire. To get an accurate idea of how much income you can expect from this source, it's important to understand the complex rules of the system. The more you know, the less likely you'll be to make decisions that could reduce your or your spouse's benefits.

Who Can Collect?

In general, you're "covered" by social security if you've worked in a job—either as an employee or as a self-employed person—where you pay social security taxes. You become "fully insured" for retirement benefits once you've met the earnings requirements over 40 quarters—generally ten years of covered work.

Once you turn 62, you become eligible to start receiving benefits. But if you wait until the "normal retirement age," which is currently 65, to apply for benefits, you'll receive more. Starting after the year 2000, the normal retirement age for social security benefits will gradually increase until it reaches 67 in the year 2027. This affects people born in 1938 and later. The table on page 16 shows the normal retirement age by year of birth.

Year of Birth	Normal Retirement Age
1937 or earlier	65
1938	65 and two months
1939	65 and four months
1940	65 and six months
1941	65 and eight months
1942	65 and ten months
1943-54	66
1955	66 and two months
1956	66 and four months
1957	66 and six months
1958	66 and eight months
1959	66 and ten months
1960 and later	67

Although the age for receiving full social security benefits is rising, eligibility for medicare—the federally funded health-care plan for seniors—still begins at age 65. But the age for qualifying for medicare benefits may also be raised in the future, as part of efforts to save the medicare program from going broke, so keep an eye on developments in Washington.

Currently the law still gives people born in 1937 or earlier the option of applying for social security benefits at age 62 with benefits reduced by 20%. But for people born in 1938 and later, as the table on page 17 shows, that reduction gradually increases to 30%.

Although starting early means a smaller benefit, it also means getting more checks than those who wait until 65. The benefits you collect between ages 62 and 65 give you a head start; it will take 12 years for someone with full benefits to make up the difference. And if you invest the money you take in early on, you'll be even farther ahead.

Year of Birth	Retirement Benefit at Age 62
1937 or earlier	80.0%
1938	79.2
1939	78.3
1940	77.5
1941	76.7
1942	75.8
1943-54	75.0
1955	74.2
1956	73.3
1957	72.5
1958	71.7
1959	70.8
1960 and later	70.0

Estimating Your Benefit

The formula the Social Security Administration (SSA) uses to calculate benefits is extremely complicated. Basically, the SSA takes your earnings for 35 years (up to the maximum earnings level for each year), adjusts them for wage inflation to make past earnings comparable to the level of earnings today and then calculates a monthly average. If you haven't worked that long, years of zero earnings are added to get 35 years. This, of course, has the effect of reducing your average monthly earnings figure.

Then a three-part formula is applied to the average to compute your benefit. Your benefit is a percentage of the average; the lower your income, the higher the percentage. Social security replaces about 42% of income for the average wage earner and 25% to 28% for people at the maximum earnings level.

Listed here are the approximate monthly benefits you can expect to collect if you retire at the normal retirement age:

Estimated Monthly Social Security Benefits at Normal Retirement Age

Your Age in 1996	Your Earnings in 1995				
	$20,000	$30,000	$40,000	$50,000	$61,200 or more*
45 You	$ 786	$ 1,053	$ 1,201	$ 1,326	$ 1,457
With Spouse**	1,179	1,579	1,801	1,989	2,185
55 You	786	1,053	1,192	1,287	1,369
With Spouse**	1,179	1,579	1,788	1,930	2,053
65 You	785	1,047	1,151	1,211	1,248
With Spouse**	1,177	1,570	1,726	1,816	1,872

Source: Social Security Administration. The accuracy depends on the pattern of your past and future earnings. In this table, earnings are assumed to grow at 4% per year in the future.
* *Earnings equal to or greater than the Social Security wage base from age 22 through the year before retirement.*
** *Your spouse is assumed to be the same age as you to receive a 50% spousal benefit. Your spouse may qualify for more based on his or her own record.*

As you can see in the table, a 45-year-old earning $40,000 can expect to collect about $1,201 a month when he or she retires at 66, the normal retirement age for people born 1943-54. If he or she was married and the spouse had a lower salary, they would collect at least $1,801 between them. (See page 19 for more on benefits for married couples.)

Here's another point to keep in mind about social security benefits: They are indexed to inflation. Every year, benefits are automatically increased based on the changes in the consumer price index (CPI). Your benefit will continue to rise as long as you collect. A word of caution: Scaling back the increase in cost-of-living adjustments is one tactic many in Congress would like to use to address long-term financial problems facing the system. Therefore it's likely that these increases will be lower in the future, but *some* automatic increase is certainly better than none.

If you want a better idea of what you can expect from social security based on your earnings thus far, call 800–772–1213 and ask for a *Request for Earnings and Benefit Estimate Statement* (Form 7004-SM). Fill it out and send it in; you'll receive a response in six weeks or less. The statement will show your complete earnings history and an estimate of what your benefits will be at 62, at normal retirement age and if you wait until age 70 to apply. You can also request an estimate statement on the World Wide Web (www.ssa.gov). People 60 and older can get an estimate of benefits over the phone.

Understanding Benefits for Couples

Once you begin collecting social security benefits, your spouse can also receive benefits based on your work history, even if he or she never worked in a job covered by social security. Your spouse can begin collecting benefits at age 62, but will get about 25% more if he or she waits until the normal retirement age. (The normal retirement age for nonworking spouses born in 1938 or later will increase on the same schedule as the age for workers.) At that time, your spouse will generally get about half of what you receive. As a couple, you'll collect 150% of what you're eligible for on your own.

If your spouse's work is covered by social security, he or she will get a benefit based on his or her actual earnings *or* 50% of your benefit, whichever is greater. If one spouse wants to retire at 65 while the other continues working, he or she can start collecting benefits based on his or her own record. When the other spouse retires, the already retired spouse can switch to receiving 50% of the other's benefit, if that will be more. But if one of you starts collecting reduced benefits before the normal retirement age, your benefit will stay reduced, even if you switch to 50% of your spouse's benefit when he or she retires.

Social security usually provides survivors' benefits to the spouses of deceased covered workers. A spouse can claim widow(er)'s benefits as long as she or he is entitled to a benefit based on her or his work record that is *less* than the amount the deceased spouse was entitled to, and she or he is 60 or older (or disabled and between ages 50 and 59). If the surviving spouse waits until age 65 to start collecting benefits, she or he should receive 100% of the deceased spouse's larger benefit, but as stated earlier, collecting at ages 60 to 64 will mean receiving a lesser amount.

However, if you qualify for benefits on your own record and your spouse dies before you reach age 65, you can start collecting your own benefit as early as 62 and delay the widow(er)'s benefit (if you qualify for it) until age 65. In that case, you will receive 100% of your deceased spouse's benefit.

How Your Benefits Will Be Taxed

In recent years, figuring out how much of your social security benefits are taxable has become incredibly complex. Fortunately, for most people benefits are tax free. But for some people, up to 50% of their benefits can be taxed, and for others, up to 85% of benefits are taxable.

The percentage of your benefits that will be taxed is based on how much "provisional income" you have in retirement. Provisional income is your adjusted gross income (from your tax return) plus 50% of your social security benefits plus 100% of any tax-free interest income.

If your provisional income is $25,000 or less on a single return or $32,000 or less on a married filing jointly return, your benefits won't be taxed. But if your provisional income is $25,001 to $34,000 (single) or $32,001 to $44,000 (married, joint return), up to 50% of your benefits can be taxed. And if your income exceeds $34,000 (single) or $44,000 (joint), another formula kicks in and you'll pay taxes on anywhere from 50% to 85% of benefits. (If you are married and file separately, your threshold amount is $0 and you'll almost definitely have to pay taxes on 85%.)

In case you were wondering, these income thresholds are *not* increased each year based on inflation. Therefore inflation pushes more and more people into the group whose benefits are taxed each year. Keep that in mind when making projections about your income in retirement.

The Late Retirement Bonus

If you delay applying for benefits beyond the normal retirement age, you earn credits that will increase your benefit when you finally do start collecting. You'll get a late retirement bonus of up to 8% for each year you put off collecting benefits after age 65. The bonus amount increases on the following schedule, which will provide future retirees with attractive incentives for delaying social security benefits:

Year of birth	Annual Bonus*
1931-32	5.0%
1933-34	5.5
1935-36	6.0
1937-38	6.5
1939-40	7.0
1941-42	7.5
1943 or later	8.0

For every year you work beyond the normal retirement age.

The bonus is also compounded since each year's bonus is figured on the base benefit plus any bonuses already earned. Basically, Uncle Sam is offering you a guaranteed return of up to 8% (on top of inflation adjustments) if you agree to leave your social security money untapped for a few years.

Continuing to Work While You Collect

There are limits on how much money you can earn in retirement and still collect your full social security benefits. If your earned income exceeds these limits, your benefits will be reduced, in addition to being taxed. But earned income includes only pay from a job; it does *not* include pensions, retirement pay or deferred compensation; payments from certain tax-exempt trust funds such as profit sharing, bond purchase or annuity; dividend and interest from investments and capital gains (unless you're in the brokerage business); workers' compensation and unemployment insurance; or veterans training pay.

Here are the earnings limits for 1997: If you're 62 to 64, you lose $1 in benefits for every $2 of earned income you have above $8,640. If you're 65 to 69, $1 in benefits is withheld for every $3 over $13,500. Those 70 and older can earn as much as they want without losing any social security benefits.

The good news is the earning limits for those 65 to 69 got a big boost from Congress, meaning people in that age bracket will soon be able to earn a lot more without losing benefits. Normally, the limits are adjusted upward each year according to the growth in average wages. But the limit for the 65 to 69 group will follow this accelerated schedule for the next five years:

Year	Earnings Limit
1998	$14,500
1999	15,500
2000	17,000
2001	25,000
2002	30,000

After 2002, the 65 to 69 earnings limit will go back to being indexed to the growth in average wages.

If you plan to continue working at least part-time in retirement, these limits should factor into your planning. If you find that you earn more than the limit and have enough income to live on, you'll probably be better off if you don't start collecting social security until you reach age 70 or stop working altogether.

Keep in mind that even if you earn too much to receive social security benefits after you reach 65, you're still eligible for full medicare benefits if you otherwise qualify.

For more information about social security:
- *Mercer Guide to Social Security and Medicare,* by Dale Detlefs, Robert Myers and Robert Treanor. ($12.50. Send a check to William M. Mercer, Inc., Social Security Division,

1500 Meidinger Tower, Louisville, KY 40202).
- The Social Security Administration (800–772–1213) offers a number of free booklets about how the system works including *Understanding Social Security, When You Get Social Security Retirement or Survivors Benefits* and *Social Security...What Every Woman Should Know.*
- *Social Security Manual* ($16.50 plus $5 shipping and handling; The National Underwriter Company, Customer Service Department, 505 Gest Street, Cincinnati, OH 45203; 800–543–0874).
- You can also get information about the various benefits programs on the World Wide Web (www.ssa.gov).

Chapter 3

Saving on Your Own

The third piece of the retirement income puzzle—one that's becoming increasingly important in this era of shrinking pensions and limits on social security—is the saving you do on your own. An important point to remember when considering the best ways to set aside money for retirement is that you should take full advantage of all the retirement plans your employer offers, particularly a 401(k) with a matching program, before you start salting money away in these other types of retirement accounts.

Individual Retirement Accounts

Although there is a great deal of confusion on this issue, most workers can still contribute as much as $2,000 to an individual retirement account (IRA) and deduct the contribution from their taxable income. If you're in the 28% tax bracket, a $2,000 deduction reduces your federal tax bill by $560. And even if you can't deduct contributions, the Roth IRA (page 56), which was created in the Taxpayer Relief Act of 1997, makes nondeductible IRAs virtually irresistible.

For the original, now called regular IRAs, the right to deduct contributions is phased out for some taxpayers. If you are covered by a retirement plan at work, your right to a deduction is phased out as your adjusted gross income (AGI)—basically your income before subtracting exemptions and deductions—rises from $30,000 to $40,000 for single returns and from $50,000 to $60,000 on joint returns (see the table, opposite). The phase-out zones will increase in the future.

If your adjusted gross income is:		You may take an IRA deduction of:
Single return	Joint return	
Up to $30,000	Up to $50,000	$2,000
31,000	51,000	1,800
32,000	52,000	1,600
33,000	53,000	1,400
34,000	54,000	1,200
35,000	55,000	1,000
36,000	56,000	800
37,000	57,000	600
38,000	58,000	400
39,000	59,000	200
40,000	60,000	0

On a joint return reporting an AGI of $55,000, for example, each spouse could write off up to $1,000 of IRA contributions, assuming each had compensation of at least $1,000 during the year.

Until 1998, if one spouse was covered by a retirement plan at work, the other spouse was automatically considered covered for purposes of the deduction phase-out. Now a noncovered spouse can contribute and deduct up to $2,000 a year in a regular IRA, as long as the couples' AGI on their joint return is under $150,000.

Although you generally may not contribute more to an IRA than you receive as compensation for a job, there is an exception if your husband or wife does not have a job. In that case, you may open a spousal IRA for him or her, separate from your own IRA, and contribute up to $2,000 a year to that account.

Whether or not you qualify to deduct your IRA contributions, you should take advantage of the IRA tax shelter. Money you put in the account—deductible or not—grows tax-deferred. With the regular IRA, no taxes are due until you withdraw funds from the account. That can help you outperform investments on which the interest and dividends are taxed every year.

The new Roth IRA may make the matter of deductibility moot for most taxpayers. It's called a "backloaded" IRA because the tax breaks come at the end of the line rather than at the beginning. Contributions cannot be deducted, but all withdrawals are tax-free—as long as the money is withdrawn after you are 59½ years old and after the account has been opened for at least four calendar years after the year it was opened. (Actually, unlike regular IRAs, you can withdraw funds at any time—up to the total of your contributions to the account—without tax or penalty.)

Other advantages of a Roth over a regular IRA: You are never required to withdraw funds from a Roth, whereas you must start tapping a regular IRA when you reach age 70½; and a Roth that is left to your heirs goes to them tax-free, while someone who inherits a regular IRA must pay tax on withdrawals (except to the extent they represent your nondeductible contributions).

The right to contribute to a Roth IRA is phased out as AGI rises between $95,000 and $110,000 for single filers and between $150,000 and $160,000 for couples who file joint returns. You can choose between an old-style IRA and a Roth—or have a combination—but you can't contribute more than $2,000 a year to your IRAs.

If your choice is between a Roth and a non-deductible regular IRA, it's a no-brainer. The Roth wins because withdrawals are tax-free. Financially, the Roth will beat a deductible IRA in almost all cases, too, and it's a clear winner in terms of simplicity. A real appeal of the Roth will be to workers who have forsaken the IRA because they were no longer allowed to deduct contributions.

You can open a Roth IRA at banks, mutual funds or brokerages that offer regular IRAs. If you have an old-style IRA, you'll be confronted with the decision of whether to convert it to a Roth IRA—so all future earnings could be tax-free. The price of admission is steep: to convert you must pay tax on all the money that, so far, has escaped tax inside your old IRA. You'll need to do some figuring to see if paying sooner rather than later makes sense for you. Basically, it can pay off if you are likely to be in the same or a higher tax bracket when you tap the IRA than you are now.

To encourage taxpayers to convert, Congress decided that those who make the switch during 1998 will get to spread the tax bill on the old IRA over four years.

While the tax breaks are the carrots to encourage investors to save for retirement, IRAs also carry a stick: As with 401(k)s, if you withdraw funds before age 59½, there is generally a 10% penalty. There are exceptions. Early withdrawals are permitted penalty-free to pay medical expenses that exceed 7.5% of your AGI, health insurance premiums during lengthy periods of unemployment, and college bills for yourself, your spouse, your child or your grandchild. You can also withdraw up to $10,000 penalty-free to help pay for a first home for yourself, your spouse, child, grandchild, parent or grandparent. (That $10,000 is a lifetime limit, not an annual one.)

Beware: Although approved early withdrawals will be free of the 10% penalty, they will be fully taxed in your top bracket (except to the extent the withdrawal represents nondeductible contributions). A big chunk of the withdrawal would go to federal and state taxes rather than toward a down payment on a house or tuition. And, remember that the point of your IRA is to save for your retirement.

You can also avoid the penalty by making a series of roughly equal withdrawals tied to your life expectancy, as long as you continue to make them for at least five consecutive years *and* until you're at least 59½.

With regular IRAs, once you turn 70½, you're *required* to begin withdrawing at least a minimum amount (based on your life expectancy) each year from your IRA to avoid a stiff 50% penalty.

Keoghs and SEPs for the Self-employed

People who are self-employed, or people who do a little moonlighting or free-lance work, have more retirement-saving options to consider. These vehicles are designed to allow people who work for themselves to set up their own "pensions."

Keoghs

These retirement plans have many similarities to IRAs: Contributions are deductible, earnings grow tax-deferred and there's a 10% early-withdrawal penalty. However, there are important differences, too. The Keoghs that are available if you have self-employment income have annual contribution limits much higher than the IRA's $2,000 cap. You can also deduct Keogh contributions no matter how high your income and regardless of whether you or your spouse are covered by an employer's retirement plan. The contribution limits vary depending on how much self-employment income you have and what kind of Keogh you select. The most popular Keogh allows you to contribute up to $30,000 per year. As with IRAs, the money is taxable when you take it out of the plan.

You can have a Keogh in addition to an IRA, but a Keogh counts as an employer-provided retirement plan for purposes of the IRA deductibility restrictions. If you have employees, establishing a Keogh plan requires that you make contributions for them as well as yourself. But this discussion assumes that no employees are involved.

Keogh plans come in three basic flavors:

- ***Profit-sharing defined-contribution Keogh.*** This is the most flexible plan because it lets you decide every year how much you want to contribute. You can even skip a year. You can contribute as much as 15% of your net self-employment earnings, up to an annual maximum of $24,000 (in 1998). However, you can't just contribute 15% of the net income reported on your Schedule C business return. You need to adjust your net income for the Keogh contribution itself; multiplying the figure by 13.0435% accomplishes that. So to figure your maximum contribution, take your self-employment income and subtract your self-employment tax deduction (50% of the self-employment tax you pay). Then multiply the remainder by 13.0435%. Fortunately, the IRS provides a table that calculates the maximum contribution for you in Publication 560, Retirement Plans for the Self-Employed.

- ***Money-purchase defined-contribution Keogh.*** This plan has a $30,000 annual limit and permits you to save up to 20% of your self-employment income. Although this type of Keogh gives you a bigger potential deduction, it comes with a restriction: You're required to make the same fixed-percentage-of-income contribution each year. So if your plan calls for a 20% contribution, you'll have to put that much in every year, even when you have a bad year and can't really afford it.

If you'd like to be able to contribute more than the profit-sharing Keogh allows, but want to avoid that restriction, open one of each of these types of Keoghs. That way you could put 7%, for example, in the money-purchase Keogh every year and put anywhere from zero to 13% in the profit-sharing Keogh. In any given year you could contribute as little as 7% or as much as 20% to your plans.

- ***Defined-Benefit Keogh.*** This offers the biggest potential tax shelter, but it's also the most complicated. With it, you decide how big a benefit you want to receive each year after you retire. Your contributions—up to 100% of your self-employment income—are based on how much you must set aside each year before retirement to build a fund to pay those benefits. There are restrictions on how big your Keogh benefit can be, but they are pretty generous and are adjusted for inflation. For 1998, the limit is the average of your self-employment earnings during your three highest-earning years or $130,000, whichever is less.

This type of plan is particularly attractive to taxpayers 50 and older who want to—and can afford to—build up a big retirement fund quickly. Because this type of Keogh involves complex actuarial computations, you'll need an accountant to help you set one up. And you can expect to pay annual administrative expenses.

SEPs

Simplified Employee Pensions (SEPs) are popular among self-employed people because they involve a lot less paperwork than Keoghs. You can contribute up to 13.0435% of your net self-employment income (reduced by the self-employment tax deduction, as with Keoghs) to a SEP, up to a limit of $24,000 a year. You can change the percentage of income you contribute each year or skip contributions all together. As with a Keogh, if you have employees, you must make contributions for them as well as yourself, but this discussion assumes that's not the case.

SEPs, which are sometimes called SEP-IRAs or Super IRAs, are a hybrid between a Keogh and an IRA. Contributions go into a special individual retirement account at a bank, mutual fund, brokerage or other custodian, and you have the same investment and transfer options as with a regular IRA. Just be sure you make it clear to the financial institution that you're opening a SEP—otherwise it might try to limit your annual contributions to $2,000.

Most rules that apply to IRAs apply to SEPs as well, a key difference being that you can deduct all SEP contributions regardless of your AGI. However, like a Keogh, a SEP is considered an employer-provided plan for purposes of the IRA-deduction restrictions.

Choosing an Annuity

Annuities are investments designed to offer an income stream for life with some tax savings along the way. You have a variety of options to consider when purchasing an annuity: How you pay for it; how the money is invested; when the monthly payments begin; and how long the annuity will continue to pay you.

You can either invest in an annuity with a lump sum up front (a single-premium annuity), or pay in gradually over a number of years (a flexible-premium annuity). The company offering the annuity invests the money for you and it grows untaxed until you withdraw it—either in a lump sum or in a series of payments over a specified period of time. This tax-sheltered growth is an annuities' chief attraction.

The two main types of annuities are *fixed* and *variable*. *Fixed annuities* pay a fixed rate for a certain period of time. *Variable annuities* offer you a choice of investments and the chance for a higher (or lower) rate of return, depending on how the investments perform. The best choice for you depends on your risk tolerance and your goals.

Fixed Annuities

You can buy fixed annuities from insurance agents, financial planners, brokers or banks. When you can begin receiving payouts from the annuity is determined by what type you choose. A *deferred annuity*, which lets you put money in now and begin receiving payments at a future date, is the more appropriate choice for someone who's planning for retirement, while an *immediate annuity*—you make a lump-sum payment and immediately begin receiving monthly payouts—makes more sense for retirees who may need more current income.

With a fixed annuity, you're guaranteed a specific interest rate for a certain period of time, usually one to five years. At the end of that period, a renewal rate is declared for the next period. Your renewal rate could be higher or lower than your initial rate. There's a minimum guaranteed rate, commonly 3% to 5%. Some annuities offer bailout rates: If your rate drops below that, you can get out with no penalty. You might earn about a half a percentage point less on an annuity with that feature.

Before you buy an annuity for its good current rate, get a copy of the company's history of renewal rates to check its record for paying long-term investors. You should be wary of an annuity offering a rate two or three percentage points higher than average. To find out the current average interest rate for the type of fixed annuity you're considering, get a copy of *Comparative Annuity Reports* ($10; 916–487–7863).

Annuities paying higher rates often fall into one of these categories:

- **Bonus rates** are paid for the first year only. The rate you earn after that can be one or two percentage points lower. If the lower rate is competitive, then that annuity is still a good deal. Sometimes you don't get the bonus rate unless you stay in the contract for a certain length of time or annuitize (start receiving regular payouts) with the company.
- **Market-value-adjusted rate** annuities pay a higher rate to entice you into taking on some market risk. The surrender value of your annuity goes up and down with interest rates. If you want to get out after a few years and rates

have gone down, the company will give you credit against any penalty charges. But if rates have gone up, you'll pay the penalty.

Another important point: Fixed annuities are only as safe as the insurance company that's offering them, so it's vital to contract with only the highest-rated companies. Check a company's grades with several rating agencies. If A.M. Best gives the company an A+ or A++ rating, check with two of the other rating agencies. They include Standard & Poor's, Moody's Investors Service and Duff & Phelps. An AA from any two of these companies, in addition to a high rating from Best, should indicate that the company is sound.

Most large libraries have S&P's or Moody's ratings in their reference sections, and a full-service insurance agency should have the Best guide. You can also call the rating agencies directly. Best (908–439–2200) will give you the identification number for the company you're interested in. You then call the "Bestline" (900–555–2378) and pay $2.95 per call plus $4.95 per rating. S&P's (212–208–1527), Moody's (212–553–0377) and Duff & Phelps (312–368–3157) will give you a single rating over the phone for free.

It's also possible to check Standard & Poor's and Duff & Phelps's insurer ratings in the Insurance News Network on the World Wide Web at www.insure.com.

Variable Annuities

This type of annuity is kind of like an insurance-coated mutual fund—you can choose to invest your money in stocks, a mixture of stocks and bonds or many of the other investment options available through mutual funds. Variable annuities have their strong points, but they're often sold based on claims that aren't as good as they sound. These points are frequently touted:

- A variable annuity allows you to invest in mutual-fund-like "subaccounts" and defer the taxes on earnings until you start withdrawing the money.
- The insurance aspect, which gives variable annuities their tax-deferred status, is a guaranteed "death benefit." If you

die during the accumulation phase (before you annuitize or start making withdrawals), your heirs will get at least the amount of your original investment, even if your subaccounts have lost money.

The other side of the coin is that the tax-deferral and death benefit guarantee come at a price: The average annual fee is 2%—nearly twice what you'd pay for many mutual funds—and you'll also pay yearly contract charges of around $26. If you die with money in the annuity and your heirs get the death benefit, they'll owe income taxes on all the accumulated earnings. If your money had been invested in mutual funds or other securities instead, they wouldn't owe any taxes on the gains because their tax basis would be "stepped-up" to the value of the securities at the time of your death.

But if you are willing to invest aggressively—such as in stocks or high-yielding bonds—and you're still at least seven to ten years from retirement, a good, low-fee variable annuity might be right for you. The best variable annuities offer a variety of subaccounts managed by well-known mutual fund companies. And unlike an IRA, 401(k), Keogh or SEP, *any* money, not just earned income, can enjoy tax-deferred growth in a variable annuity.

With either a fixed or variable annuity, there's a 10% penalty on money you take out before you're 59½. In addition, most annuities have company-imposed penalty periods, usually no longer than seven years after purchase, during which you forfeit a percentage of your earnings if you take out more than 10% of your money. You shouldn't lose any of your principal, but check with the company to be sure.

Annuity Payout Plans

When you need to start taking money out, you can make systematic withdrawals based on your own schedule or you can annuitize. To annuitize, you roll the accumulated value of your account into an immediate annuity with the same company (or a different company, if you wish). Then you select how you will receive the money from among a number of payout plans. The following are your major alternatives, listed in order from those producing the largest periodic pay-

ments to those producing the smallest:
- ***Life-only annuity*** guarantees a stipulated monthly income for life. No payments are made to anyone after your death. It provides the largest amount of income for your dollar and is recommended for a person who needs the maximum amount of income and either has no dependents or has taken care of them through other means.
- ***Life annuity with period certain*** gives you an income for the remainder of your life. If you die within a certain period after you start receiving income, usually ten or 20 years, your beneficiary receives regular payments for the balance of the period. These provide somewhat lower benefits than life-only annuities but do ensure that the family continues to receive income in the event of premature death.
- ***Installment-refund annuity*** also provides income for life. But if you die before you have received as much money as you paid in, your beneficiary receives regular installments until the total payments equal that amount.
- ***Joint and survivor (J&S) annuity*** guarantees payments to you and one or more survivors until the last one dies. You have several options with J&S annuities. Here are two of the most common: Joint and survivor 100% guarantees payments over your lifetime, and your survivor gets the same amount after you die. Joint and survivor 50% guarantees payments over your lifetime, but when you die your survivor's benefit is cut 50%. Because this pays a reduced benefit after your death, the payments during your lifetime are greater with J&S 50% than they are with J&S 100%.

Your tax bill on annuity payouts depends on whether the money you invested in the immediate annuity was "qualified" or "nonqualified." Qualified money is rolled over from a tax-deferred vehicle such as a pension plan, deferred annuity or IRA. Non-qualified money is after-tax savings, maybe from a CD or savings account. The payouts from an annuity funded with qualified money are fully taxable. For non-qualified money, only the portion of your income that is interest, not principal, is taxed.

Part Two

Taking Stock of Where You Are

Now that you have a better understanding of pensions, Social Security and retirement savings accounts, it's time to take a good look at where you stand. This section will lead you through the process of determining how much income you'll need to afford the retirement you want and where you are in terms of reaching that goal.

Chapter 4

What You'll Need

A recent survey by the Keyport Life Insurance Company indicated that 43% of working people don't know how much money they will need to maintain the standard of living they want in retirement. A recent Gallup poll of 30- to 49-year-olds showed that 74% of them were worried about not having enough money to live comfortably in retirement.

If you see yourself in those statistics, now's the time to get a good fix on how much income you'll need in retirement. Worrying about it won't motivate you to start saving (or saving more), but having a clear idea of how much money it will take to reach your goals may just give you the discipline you need.

Tracking Your Spending

The first step in any type of planning for your financial future is determining exactly what you're doing with your money *now*. The good news is that if you have a detailed budget and stick to it, or you keep track of your spending and finances with money-management software, this first step will be easy for you. But if you have only a vague sense of where your money goes, you won't be able to create a realistic retirement plan until you've got a handle on your spending.

Start by keeping track of all your expenditures for two or three months. Include everything, from bills and large purchases to what you spend on your morning coffee and muffin. Keep a small notepad with you for writing down each expenditure and then record each day's outlays in a ledger book—or with money-management software, such as *Quicken* or *Managing Your Money*—organizing them into spending categories. For expenses you pay annually or quarterly—insurance premiums, for example—calculate what one month's payment would be. The worksheet on the following page can help you get started; add or subtract categories to reflect your situation.

Once you have a few months' of data, you'll have an accurate picture of your spending habits. You'll be able to create a budget and target areas in which you can cut back in order to put more into savings and investments, or to pay off debts. And if you continue to track your spending over the years, you'll be able to determine at what rate your expenses tend to increase over time. This will help you come up with a ballpark figure for what some of your expenses—ones that are unlikely to be changed much by your retirement, such as food, personal care and utilities—are likely to be when you reach retirement.

Estimating Your Retirement Income Needs

Although your detailed budget can be used as the basis for determining roughly how much income you're likely to need in retirement, many people find that their spending shifts somewhat in retirement. They may find that they spend more in some categories, such as health care and travel, and less on clothing, public transportation and other work-related expenses.

You've probably heard that you will need about 80% of your before-retirement income to maintain your standard of living as a retiree. But that rule of thumb may not apply to everyone. A more precise way to predict your income needs in retirement is to adjust your budget according to lifestyle changes you expect to make in retirement, and then project how that amount will increase in the future due to inflation.

Your Monthly Budget

Fixed Expenses

Mortgage or rent	$ _____
Property taxes	_____
Car payments	_____
Other installment payments	_____
Credit-card payments	_____
Insurance: Auto	_____
Homeowners	_____
Life	_____
Health & other	_____
Savings or investments	_____
Subtotal for fixed expenses	$ _____

Variable Expenses

Food (groceries & dining out)	$ _____
Utilities: Gas or oil	_____
Electricity	_____
Telephone	_____
Water & sewer	_____
Home maintenance (furnishings & improvements)	_____
Car (gas, oil & repairs)	_____
Public transportation	_____
Day care/baby-sitting	_____
Medical & dental co-payments or bills not covered by insurance	_____
Clothing (including dry cleaning)	_____
Personal care (haircuts, health club membership, etc.)	_____
Educational expenses	_____
Entertainment, recreation	_____
Gifts	_____
Charitable giving	_____
Miscellaneous	_____
Subtotal of variable expenses	$ _____
Subtotal of fixed expenses	$ _____
Total	$ _____

To get you started thinking about how your spending might change in retirement, this pie chart shows how the average 65+ household spends its money:

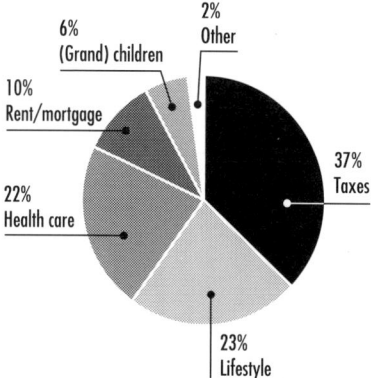

Source: The Equitable Nest Egg Study, 1995. Polled a total of 1,200 individuals with a household income of $50,000 or more.

As you can see, for many people the biggest chunk goes for taxes and lifestyle expenses, such as travel and entertainment, and health care is also a big expense.

How *your* retirement budget breaks down will depend on a number of personal factors. If you want to retire to a big, beautiful home on the beach instead of staying put or scaling down to a smaller home, housing may be a larger piece of your pie. In addition, *where* you live in retirement—what part of the country and what type of community—will also make a difference in your spending. If you choose to live in a small city, town or rural area after you retire, you will probably need less income than you would living in a large city or metropolitan area—particularly the more expensive ones along the east and west coasts. And what state and county you live in will affect how much taxes you pay.

Once you've decided what parts of your current budget you will probably drop, add to or cut-back on in retirement, adjust the figures accordingly. What you come up with may be more or less than 80% of the amount you're currently spending. To figure out the percentage you'll need, divide your "retirement budget" total by your current budget total.

Kiplinger • Successful Retirement **39**

Then multiply that amount by 100 to convert it to a percentage. For example, if your current budget total is about $63,000 and after you've made adjustments it looks like your retirement budget will total $60,000—you don't expect to be able to spend less in very many categories—the retirement income percentage you should use is 95%. ($60,000 ÷ divided by $63,000 = 0.95; 100 x 0.95 = 95%.)

If you want to take a faster, simpler approach, just multiply your current budget total by 80% to find your target retirement income in today's dollars.

Now you need to convert that estimate of your target retirement income into future dollars. To adjust that figure to account for 4% annual inflation between now and when you retire, use the appropriate inflation factor from the table on page 41 that corresponds to the number of years you have until retirement (5 years to go, 1.22; 10 years to go, 1.48; etc.).

Plug your numbers into the following equation: Target income in today's dollars $_____ x inflation factor _____ = $_____, target retirement income in future dollars.

Take for example a 45-year-old couple, Brian and Barbara Boomer, who has a current annual income of $70,000. They determined that their retirement budget would call for $63,000 in annual income—90% of their current amount. Assuming they're planning to retire in 20 years at age 65, their target income in future dollars is $137,970.

Keep close track of the inflation rate. If it moves higher than 4% over a sustained period, you'll have to adjust how much you'll need. And as your situation changes in the future—you change jobs, move to another area or lose your spouse due to death or divorce, for example—you should recalculate your estimate.

Factoring in Post-retirement Inflation

The figure you calculated above can now serve as an estimate of how much income you'll need to maintain the standard of living you want in retirement. But that estimate only indicates how much income you'll need in your *first year* of retirement. To complete the picture, you need to figure how much more income you'll need each year as inflation continues to cause prices to go up after you retire.

Assuming a 4% annual rate of inflation, you can use the following multipliers to see how your income needs will increase as the years go by:

Effect of 4% inflation over...

Year	Multiplier
5	1.22
10	1.48
15	1.80
20	2.19
25	2.67
30	3.24

Looking at the Boomer couple again, if they will need $137,970 in their first year of retirement, they will need $248,346 after 15 years (137,970 x 1.80) and $368,380 after 25 years of retirement (assuming their lifestyles don't change that much as they age).

If those figures sound frightening, don't panic until you've gone through the rest of this booklet and seen how your income and investments will continue to grow over the years as well.

The key to maintaining a level of income that will allow you to live the way you choose throughout retirement is to make sure that your income from investments and other sources will keep pace with inflation. Social security benefits get an annual inflation increase, as discussed earlier, but most private pensions don't. That's why it's just as important after retirement as it is before to invest your savings to earn an overall return that will outpace inflation. We'll discuss how to select appropriate investments and make asset allocation decisions in Part 3.

Chapter 5

What You'll Have

Before you start feeling completely overwhelmed by how much income you'll need to fund the retirement you've been planning, let's take a close look at what you've got so far. You already know that some, perhaps a good portion, of the income you'll need will come from your pension and social security. The remainder will likely come from your investment portfolio and perhaps from some sort of free-lance or part-time work, if that's something you see yourself doing.

Totaling Up Your Income and Assets

Depending on how much serious planning and saving you've done thus far, you're either looking forward to or dreading this next step. Look at it this way: You'll either be pleased about where you stand or you'll have information that will motivate you to start saving in earnest.

The worksheet on page 43 can serve as a prompt to help you tabulate everything you've accumulated so far. If you're unsure of amounts in some categories, use your best estimate now and come back later when you've gathered exact figures. Taking the time to track them down now will give you an excuse to put off finishing what you've started. (Add your and your spouse's benefits or assets together and enter the total wherever applicable.)

Retirement Assets to Date

I. Estimated Regular Annual Income in Retirement

Annual social security benefit
(estimate from SSA) $ _____

Defined-benefit pension annual benefit
(estimate from plan) $ _____

Other sources of regular annual income
(military pension, annuity) $ _____

**Total Annual Regular Income
in Retirement** $ _____

II. Current Nest Egg

Retirement Account Assets

Defined-contribution plan total
(401(k), 457, ESOP, etc.) $ _____
Profit-sharing account total _____
Tax-sheltered annuity total (403(b) plan) _____
Individual retirement accounts total (IRAs) _____
Keogh account total _____

Other Assets and Savings

Bank accounts $ _____
Money-market funds _____
Certificates of deposit (CDs) _____
Treasury securities _____
Mutual funds _____
Stocks _____
Bonds _____
Real estate investments _____
Business interests _____
Other _____

Current Total Nest Egg $ _____

Determining Your Income Gap

The next step is to look at the difference between the amount of income you'll have, which you totaled up in the top portion of the worksheet on page 43, and the amount of income you'll need according to your calculations from the last section.

Take again the example of the 45-year-old Boomers who want to retire at 65 and currently have $70,000 in annual income. The two of them can expect to collect about $24,000 in social security benefits per year (see page 18), based on Brian receiving the maximum social security benefit and Barbara receiving a spousal benefit. Brian, who has a defined-benefit pension, currently earns $50,000 a year. Assuming it keeps pace with inflation, Brian's salary should grow to $109,500 ($50,000 x 2.19) when he retires in 2016 after 30 years with the company. He expects to collect a pension of about $49,000 per year in future dollars. (Barbara participates in a 401(k) plan. Because it's not a fixed source of income, it should not be considered here). So their total regular income at retirement from the worksheet above will be $73,000.

Now use the following equation to determine the gap between how much income they expect to need and what they'll have:

$$\underset{\substack{\text{future annual} \\ \text{income needed}}}{\$\underline{\qquad}} - \underset{\substack{\text{estimated annual} \\ \text{future income}}}{\$\underline{\qquad}} = \underset{\text{gap in future dollars}}{\$\underline{\qquad}}$$

The Boomers have figured that they'll need $137,970 in annual income and they've estimated that they'll have about $73,000 from regular sources. That leaves a retirement income gap of $64,970 in future dollars in the first year. As the years of retirement go by, their income needs will likely increase at about the rate of inflation (as shown on page 41), but only their social security benefits will get an inflation adjustment. For that reason, the gap between the income they need and what the income they have will grow as the years go by. By investing the assets tabulated in the second part of the worksheet above, plus whatever they can manage to add to that in the next 20 years, they will need to produce enough income to fill that gap when they retire, and for many years afterwards as the gap widens.

Chapter 6

Closing the Gap

Closing the gap between how much income you'll need in retirement and how much you'll have coming in from regular sources is the final piece in completing your retirement income puzzle. It may sound daunting, but let's take a look at how much income your current savings could produce and then figure out how much more you need to save in order to produce enough income to fill your retirement income gap.

Comparing Your Nest Egg with Your Needs

Using Part II of the worksheet on page 43, you added up how much of a nest egg you've accumulated thus far. Now use the table below to determine how much your current nest egg will grow between now and retirement. For example, say the Boomers have a total of $90,000 in savings for retirement, including their IRAs, Barbara's 401(k), mutual funds and other investments. They are currently earning an 8% return on that money and if that continues for the next 20

Nest Egg Growth Factors

Years to Retirement	Expected Annual Return			
	6%	8%	10%	12%
5	1.34	1.47	1.61	1.76
10	1.79	2.16	2.59	3.11
15	2.40	3.17	4.18	5.40
20	3.21	4.66	6.73	9.65

$_____ x _____ = _____
current nest egg   growth factor   nest egg at retirement

years, without adding anything to their current savings, they should have approximately $419,400 (current nest egg of $90,000 x 4.66, the growth factor for 8% return for 20 years = $419,400 future nest egg).

Will $419,400 be enough to fill the Boomers' $65,000 retirement income gap? Will your nest egg be enough to fill your gap?

To figure this out, start by breaking your annual income gap down into a monthly amount: Divide your retirement income gap by 12. For Brian and Barbara, that means they'll need another $5,417 per month ($65,000 ÷ 12). Use the following table to figure out what size nest egg the Boomers' would need to produce that much income—and how much you'll need.

Amount Needed to Generate $1,000 Per Month

Assuming principle will be reduced to zero at the end of retirement

Years in Retirement	Annual Rate of Return		
	6%	8%	10%
10	$ 90,073	$ 82,420	$ 75,670
15	118,504	104,640	93,060
20	139,581	119,550	103,620
25	155,207	129,560	110,050

Since the Boomers plan to invest in a mix of stocks and fixed-income investments and expect to earn an 8% return on their money for 20 years of retirement, they use the following calculation: $119,550 x ($5,417 ÷ 1,000) = $647,602. But if one or both of them has a history of longevity in their family, they should plan on 25 years, which means they'll need $701,827 ($129,560 x 5.417).

Now decide what return you can expect to earn on your investments in retirement—6% being appropriate for conservative, fixed-income investors and 10% applying to those who plan to invest predominantly in stocks. Then find the figure in the table where that rate of return intersects with the number of years you expect to live in retirement. In most cases, that should be *at least* 20 years if you plan on retiring at age 65. Now fill in the equation below:

$$\underset{\text{figure from table}}{\$\underline{\hspace{1in}}} \times \underset{\substack{\text{monthly shortfall} \\ \text{divided by 1,000}}}{\underline{\hspace{1in}}} = \underset{\substack{\text{preliminary} \\ \text{nest egg goal}}}{\$\underline{\hspace{1in}}}$$

But you probably noticed that this equation only gives you a "preliminary" nest egg to shoot for. That's because you need to adjust the preliminary goal to account for the fact that as inflation increases your income needs after retirement, you'll need to draw more from your nest egg each year to maintain your lifestyle. For a rough estimate of how much more you'll need to keep up with inflation, multiply your preliminary figure by 1.3 if you expect to live 20 years in retirement or multiply by 1.4 if you expect an even longer retirement.

$$\underset{\text{preliminary goal}}{\$\underline{\hspace{1in}}} \times \underset{\text{inflation factor}}{\underline{\hspace{1in}}} = \underset{\substack{\text{inflation-adjusted} \\ \text{nest-egg goal}}}{\$\underline{\hspace{1in}}}$$

For Brian and Barbara, that means they will need to aim for a nest egg of $841,883 ($647,602 x 1.3) for a 20-year retirement and $982,558 ($701,827 x 1.4) if they plan to live another 25 years after they retire.

As we calculated on page 46, without adding anything to it, their current nest egg will have grown to $419,400 by the time they're 65. If they want to continue to aim for the goal of retiring at 65 with an initial annual income of $137,970 and living into their 80s, they need to come up with a plan to accumulate *at least* $422,483 ($841,883 − $419,400) in additional savings and return on their money. That sounds like a lot of money. But on the bright side, they're nearly halfway there already.

Boosting Your Savings

For most people, the series of calculations we've just gone through will produce the same conclusion it did for Brian and Barbara Boomer: You need to save a lot more between now and when you retire. How much more? To figure that out, let's take a closer look at what the Boomers expect to be able to accomplish in the 20 years between now and when they retire.

Brian and Barbara don't know for sure how much they'll be able to save in the next 20 years, but they're concerned because they know they've only been able to accumulate $90,000 in assets up to this point. What they need to keep in mind is that they are now entering their peak earning years and may find that they are able to save more than they expect, especially after they've finished paying off their mortgage and putting their two kids through college. In addition, they haven't always earned 8% on the savings they've been accumulating. That's what they've been earning since they met with a financial planner earlier this year and reallocated their money so that it was more heavily invested in stocks—a good decision since they have another 20 years before they will have to start tapping their nest egg.

Use the following table to determine how much the Boomers will have to save per month to build another $422,483 into their nest egg and how much *you* will have to save to make up your estimated nest-egg shortfall.

Savings Target Factors

| Years | Annual Compounded Rate of Return | | | | |
to Go	6%	7%	8%	9%	10%
5	0.014322	0.013967	0.013621	0.013285	0.012958
10	0.006125	0.005813	0.005516	0.005233	0.004964
15	0.003469	0.003196	0.002943	0.002708	0.002490
20	0.002195	0.001959	0.001746	0.001554	0.001381
25	0.001471	0.001270	0.001093	0.000939	0.000804

$_____ x _____ = $_____
  nest-egg goal   savings target   monthly savings
                             factor   needed to meet goal

Looking at where 8%—the Boomers' expected annual return—and 20 years intersect, you'll find that the savings target factor they should use is 0.001746. If their goal is to accumulate another $422,483, their monthly savings target is $738 ($442,483 x 0.001746).

Is that a doable savings goal for the Boomers? How realistic is the savings goal you came up with? Go back to the spending breakdown you created on page 38. See how much additional saving you could do each month by cutting back here and there on unnecessary expenses. Remember that the sooner you get started the better. If you put off boosting your savings for a few years, the amount you need to save will climb in the meantime.

Another way to make your savings goal more manageable is to boost the annual return you earn on your portfolio. Investing more of your money in stocks or stock mutual funds could bring your annual rate of return up to 10%. In the Boomers' case, that would bring their monthly savings target down to $583. It would be even less if they reallocated their current $90,000 nest egg to earn 10% as well. Averaging a 10% annual return, that $90,000 will grow to $605,700 by the time they reach 65. Earning 12%, it would grow to $868,500. Averaging more than a 10% annual return over 20 years is not unreasonable, if you have enough of your money in domestic and international equity holdings.

Adjusting Your Goals

After fiddling around with the numbers a bit, you may find that saving more or taking more risk with your money by investing a larger portion in stocks may still leave you short of your goal. If you find that you just won't be able to save enough at this point no matter what you do, it's time to consider making changes in your plans and rethink your retirement with a realistic idea in mind of where you stand. One or more of the following options may do the trick for you.

Sell Your Home

When you retire, you may no longer need or want a home the size of the one you have now. Selling your home and buying or renting a smaller place will probably free up a chunk of money that you can invest for more income.

Brian and Barbara Boomer's home is now worth about $175,000. In 20 years, it could be worth a lot more. And, thanks to provisions in the 1997 tax law (discussed in Chapter 10), they'll probably get to keep all the profit they make when they eventually sell.

Move to a Lower-cost Area

In addition to scaling down the size of your home, moving to a lower cost and lower tax area when you retire can make a big difference in how much income you'll actually need to live comfortably.

Once you've cut back on large expenses such as housing and taxes, you may find that saving in a number of small ways also helps you to live on less and still live comfortably. For example, retirees are usually much freer to take advantage of travel bargains by planning trips at the last minute or traveling during off-peak seasons. In addition, retirees can take advantage of the discounted prices on everything from movies to hotel accommodations to dining out that are made available to senior citizens.

Delay Retirement

Moving the year you plan to retire back another three to five years will add to your savings *and* boost the amount of pension and social security benefits you'll get when you do retire. Another option is to ease into retirement by continuing to work on a part-time basis or doing free-lance work for the first several years after you "retire." The additional income could significantly improve your retirement picture and let you put off tapping your pension and social security for a few more years. (More on working in retirement beginning on page 86.)

Chapter 7

Is Early Retirement an Option?

In 1970, 83% of men ages 55 to 64 were in the workforce; now only about 65% of men in that age group are working. In part, this trend is the result of corporate downsizing, but, in addition, many people are retiring as soon as they think they can afford it.

Is that wise? Certainly some people are able to quit working early and enjoy long and successful retirements. But for many, the financial facts of life make early retirement difficult, if not impossible. After all, retiring early means losing years of income—often your peak earning years. You'll probably have smaller pension checks and lower monthly payments from social security. And, as you've already seen, inflation makes it difficult to maintain your standard of living in retirement; the longer you're retired, the longer your money will have to last.

The Impact on Your Pension

If you have a defined-benefit pension plan, the benefit you'll receive as a retiree is based on your years of service, your age and your salary, as explained on page 9. That means you can lose a significant amount by retiring early because you won't build up as many retirement credits and your pension will likely be based on a lower salary than if you had stayed. In addition, defined-benefit plans often penalize employees further for retiring early—some plans lower pension benefits by a certain percentage for retiring before age 60 or 62, others may knock as much as 5% to 7% off the benefit for each year you are under age 65 when you retire. The following table shows how much lower your pension could be if you retire early, assuming pay raises of 5% a year under a fairly typical plan.

Age at Retirement	Average Pay Last 5 Years	Years of Service	Annual Pension Starting at Age 65*	
55	$60,000	20	$18,000	($13,500)
56	63,000	21	19,845	(15,876)
57	66,150	22	21,830	(18,555)
58	69,460	23	23,960	(21,564)
59	72,930	24	26,255	(24,942)
60	76,575	25	28,716	
61	80,405	26	31,358	
62	84,425	27	34,192	
63	88,645	28	37,230	
64	93,080	29	40,490	
65	97,735	30	43,980	

The figures in parenthesis show the effect if the annual pension is reduced by an early retirement penalty of 5% for each year between when the person retires and age 60 (25% at age 55, 20% at age 56, etc).

If you're in a defined-contribution plan, you can retire early without penalty. However, you'll still miss out on what are likely to be your peak earnings years, when you probably could contribute more than ever to your plan.

Sizing Up a Golden Handshake

Many major companies have been reducing their staffs by offering early-retirement incentives to long-term, highly paid employees. Forecasters expect large-scale buyout offers to become less common in the future, but if you find yourself being offered a "golden handshake"—another term for an early-retirement incentive package—take the time to analyze the offer carefully. In fact, because buyout offers are so complicated and because so much is at stake, you may want to have a financial planner analyze it for you. (See page 69 for more on finding a good financial planner.) The analysis will probably cost several hundred dollars, but it'll be well worth the money to know if you're getting a good deal or if you should pass up the offer.

A buyout package can include a variety of incentives. Some offer to boost your defined-benefit pension by adding three to five years or more to your tenure. That can mean an increase of as much as a third in your monthly benefit check, as you can see in the table on page 52. Or a package could include a lump-sum severance payment based on your salary and length of service—this would be taxed as regular income and could not be rolled over into an IRA. You may also get extra income to carry you over until you're eligible for social security benefits at age 62. And you can sometimes extend the health and life insurance coverage provided by your employer.

As you evaluate the offer, make sure you address these questions:

- How does your pension benefit plus the offer compare to what you'd get if you continued working until the company's normal retirement age?
- How much of your buyout package will be taxed as ordinary income? What will you have left after taxes?
- What happens if you don't accept the offer? Will salary increases and bonuses stop if you decide to stay? Try to get a feel for the situation at your company. If there's a chance that you'll be laid off in the future, you may be better off taking this offer now.
- If health insurance isn't included in your package, you need to seriously consider how you're going to get coverage for you (and maybe your spouse) while you're waiting for medicare to kick in at age 65. Federal law requires that you continue to be covered for 18 months by your employer's plan, but you'll have to pay your share and the

company's share of the cost plus an administrative fee that could be 2% or more. Trying to buy coverage on your own can be astronomically expensive, even if you go with an HMO.
- Can you afford to retire with this package or will you need to find another job? Start looking into your prospects for employment outside the company. (See page 86 for more on finding a job after you "retire.") Consider whether you have enough savings to tide you over until you find another position.

PART 3

Making Your Money Work for You

Now that you have a good sense of what you need to accomplish in terms of saving and investing, let's consider what steps you can take now and in the future to get the most benefit possible out of the assets you accumulate. The decisions you make about how to invest your savings and, eventually, how to receive your pension benefits will determine whether your carefully laid retirement plans work out the way they should. In addition, we'll explore how you may be able to plug any remaining gaps in your retirement savings by tapping the assets you've invested in your home.

CHAPTER 8

Creating an Investment Strategy

Today there are more investment options available to individual investors than ever before, and new types of investments enter the market all the time. The result of this trend: Endless possibilities for creating well-diversified investment portfolios and, at the same time, endless confusion over how to make the right choices.

This chapter provides a general overview of the basic investments available to you, some of the risks that go with them, how to lessen your exposure to risk by diversifying your investments and sample investment mixes for people in their 40s, 50s and 60s. We'll also explore the idea of getting professional help with your investing from a financial planner. You'll learn how to choose a planner who will suit your needs and act in your best interest.

Investment Options: Stocks, Bonds, Mutual Funds & Real Estate

The investments discussed here are the basic building blocks of any portfolio. Although other options are available, including some that are more complicated and difficult for an individual investor to use effectively, these should be sufficient for creating a diversified portfolio that provides you with ample exposure to the stock and fixed-income investment markets.

Stocks

When investors talk about stocks, they usually mean "common" stocks. A share of common stock represents a share of ownership in the company that issues it. A stock's price goes up and down, depending on how the company performs and how investors *think* the company will perform in the future. There are several basic, sometimes overlapping, types of common stocks that you may want to buy for your portfolio:

- ***Growth stocks*** are stocks of companies that have grown faster than the economy in the past and are expected to continue to grow rapidly in the future. Some pay dividends; others plow all their profits back into the business to maintain growth. Investors like them for their consistent earnings growth. Some stocks are considered aggressive growth because they may grow much faster than other stocks over the short term, but they are also more speculative and, therefore, riskier.

- ***Blue-chip stocks*** are generally industry leaders, such as AT&T, Coca-Cola, Kellogg, Merck and Procter & Gamble, that tend to pay decent dividends that steadily increase year after year. They generate some growth, and they offer safety and reliability. These are buy-and-hold investments for the long haul.

- ***Income stocks*** pay out higher dividends—often more than half of their profits—than do other stocks. These companies tend to be more mature, slow-growers that have stable and reliable earnings. Utility companies, for example, are one type of income stock. Share prices don't grow rapidly, but the dividend sort of cushions the price; even if the market drops as a whole, income stocks are usually less affected because investors continue to receive their dividends.

    One way to evaluate income stocks is by comparing the stocks' *dividend yields*—the annual dividend paid as a percentage of the current share price.

- ***Small-company stocks*** are riskier than blue-chip or income stocks because they are generally newer, less established companies, and there tends to be a lot of short-term volatility—sharp rising and falling—in their share prices. However, they also offer the potential for higher returns over the long term. Since 1926, small-company stocks have produced an average annual total return of 12.2% versus 10.2% for large-company stocks.

- **Foreign stocks** let you further diversify your portfolio because international markets tend to perform differently from the U.S. market. When stocks are going down here, the stock market in another country could be skyrocketing. The key is not to put too much money in any one international market; splitting up your money among several different countries reduces the effect a downturn in one market will have on your portfolio. You also have to be mindful of currency risk; if the value of the U.S. dollar goes up against other currencies while you own foreign stocks, the value of your investment will drop, regardless of what's happening with the stock price itself.

The easiest way to acquire a diversified portfolio of foreign stocks is by investing in an international stock mutual fund (see page 62).

Bonds and Other Fixed-income Investments

A bond is basically an IOU issued by a corporation or, in the case of Treasury securities, by the U.S. government. When you buy a bond, you're making a loan to the issuer, who, in turn, agrees to pay you a specified interest rate. You will be paid that fixed amount of interest until the issuer repays the loan—when the bond matures. At maturity you'll be paid the bond's face value. It's also possible to sell the bond to another investor before it matures.

However, bonds do involve taking risk. The main risk with bonds is called "interest rate risk." If interest rates fall, bond prices rise, but if rates rise, prices fall. In a falling-rate environment, you can probably sell your bond for more than you paid for it; in a rising-rate environment, the opposite is true. But if you take a buy-and-hold approach with bond investing, you'll continue to earn your fixed rate of interest and receive the face value at maturity, so price movements needn't concern you.

There are many types of bonds from which to choose:

- ***Treasuries*** are as safe as a bond gets. They are backed by the full faith and credit of the U.S. government. Interest is free from state and local income taxes and is paid semiannually, except for Treasury bills (also known as T-bills), which are discounted up front to reflect the interest due and then you receive the full face value at maturity. Treasuries are available in various maturities: *T-bills* mature in one year or less; *T-notes* typically in two, three, five or ten years; and *Treasury bonds* have 30-year maturities.

    The minimum initial purchase for T-bills is $10,000, and $5,000 for two- and three-year notes. After that, you can buy bills, notes and bonds in $1,000 increments.

- ***Corporate bonds*** are riskier than Treasury securities because they are backed only by the companies that issue them. In exchange for more risk, you get more interest, which is usually paid twice a year. To aid investors in selecting bonds from financially sound companies, rating agencies such as Standard & Poor's (S&P) and Moody's Investors Service give bonds grades. For example, AAA is S&P's top rating (see page 32 for more on the rating services). Bonds with low or no ratings are known as "junk" or high-yield bonds. Corporate bonds are usually sold in increments of $1,000 or $5,000.

- ***Zero-coupon bonds*** pay all their interest to you at maturity, with no payouts along the way, so they are issued at big discounts from face value—as much as 50% to 75%. They come in denominations as low as $1,000. A $1,000 zero yielding 7% and maturing in 18 years would cost just $285. Zeros make good long-term investments, but, unfortunately, the IRS taxes the interest year by year as it accrues. Because it doesn't make sense to pay tax on income you haven't yet received, consider buying zeros for tax-deferred accounts, such as IRAs.

- ***Foreign bonds*** issued by the governments or corporations of other countries can pay higher yields than domestic bonds. But as with foreign stocks, there's currency risk that is often difficult for individual investors to manage. For that reason, mutual funds are probably the best way to buy foreign bonds.

- **Mortgage-backed securities** aren't really bonds, but they are fixed-income investments. They offer a bit more yield than Treasuries without adding a lot of risk. These securities represent pools of home mortgages that have been made by lenders nationwide. When you buy one of the securities, you receive "pass-through" payments of interest and principal from those mortgages. These securities are guaranteed by a federal agency known as Ginnie Mae (Government National Mortgage Association or GNMA) and by two quasi-government agencies, Fannie Mae (Federal National Mortgage Association) and Freddie Mac (Federal Home Loan Mortgage Corporation). Ginnie Mae securities give you the guarantee that if a homeowner defaults, the government will make up the payments. The others are backed by those agencies' funds, not Uncle Sam's.

  The market prices of mortgage securities tend to respond more to interest-rate moves than the market prices of bonds do. That's because when interest rates drop, homeowners start refinancing their mortgages at the lower rates, cutting into the return on mortgage securities. You can buy these investments from brokers, but minimum investments run as high as $25,000. It's cheaper to get good diversification by investing in a Ginnie Mae mutual fund.

- **Municipal bonds**, or munis, are issued by states, counties, cities and other political jurisdictions and their agencies, including school districts, airport authorities and bridge and highway departments. The interest earned on these bonds is almost always exempt from federal income tax, and most states don't tax the interest on munis issued by municipal authorities within their own borders. In addition, many states don't tax muni-bond interest no matter where it comes from. Ratings on munis are the key to choosing good ones, as they are with corporate bonds. It's also wise to buy munis from different parts of the country, rather than focusing only in your state, even though you might pay state tax on out-of-state munis. A regional recession or natural disaster could cause big trouble in a portfolio that's not well diversified.

  These bonds have minimum face values of $5,000 so, again, a mutual fund or unit investment trust is the cheap-

est way to get proper diversification.
- ***Guaranteed investment contracts (GICs)*** are offered as an investment option in most 401(k) plans. Think of GICs as big certificates of deposit (CDs) that are issued by insurance companies instead of banks and don't have federal deposit insurance. The contracts usually run one to seven years. Usually 401(k) plan managers buy several GICs and create a GIC fund for the plan participants, thereby spreading the money among as many as 20 insurance companies. This is good because the major risk with GICs is that they are only as good as the insurance company that issues them. But in most states, GIC investors are covered by insurance plans similar to those that protect life insurance policies.

You may find that your 401(k) plan now offers something called a "stable value pool" (SVP), or fund, in place of traditional GICs. SVPs contain a mixture of short- and long-term fixed-income securities (such as GICs, Treasuries, mortgage-backed securities and money-market funds). They are designed to sidestep some of the drawbacks associated with GICs, including a lack of diversification and the risk of insurance company insolvency, and may be a better choice.

Mutual Funds

These extremely popular investments offer a variety of advantages, including professional management and diversification. Instead of slogging through annual reports for thousands of different companies searching for the right stocks or bonds, you can invest in a fund and let a professional do the work for a fairly reasonable fee.

Mutual funds work like this: An investment company pools money from many investors and buys a portfolio of investments meant to achieve certain goals in terms of performance and risk. Minimum investments are usually between $500 and $3,000.

Many mutual funds charge commissions to investors that range around 3% to 6%—some collect this charge up-front and others apply it if you withdraw your money from the fund within five to seven years of investing. These so-called *load funds* are sold mostly through brokers, banks and other financial advisers. Funds that don't charge commissions are usually called *no-load funds*.

Both load and no-load funds levy annual fees that typically include management fees to compensate the fund's manager and administrative fees to cover other costs of running the fund. Annual fees generally run from 0.5% to 2% of the fund's assets, depending on the company and the type of fund. Funds with annual fees toward the high end of that range are often adding in what are known as 12b-1 fees, which cover the costs of selling and distributing fund shares.

More and more types of mutual funds are created all the time; here are the most common:

- **Aggressive-growth funds** seek maximum capital gains by investing in speculative stocks and sometimes using high-risk investment techniques to maximize profits. They often buy stock in the smallest or fastest-growing companies in the market.
- **Growth funds** aim to achieve an increase in the value of your investment (capital gains) rather than pay dividends. They buy growth stocks that are expected to grow faster than average, including large, established companies and smaller, emerging firms with bright prospects for the future. They tend to be less volatile than aggressive-growth funds.
- **Growth-and-income funds** balance the objectives of long-term growth and current income. They invest primarily in companies whose stocks are rising and that have a solid record of paying dividends. Growth-and-income funds tend to be more stable than growth funds.
- **Balanced funds** work toward three objectives: To conserve investors' principal; to pay current income; and to provide long-term growth of both principal and income. They do so by investing in a mix of bonds and stocks. They are usually a bit more stable than growth-and-income funds because they are diversified into bonds.
- **International stock funds** invest most, if not all, of their funds in stocks of companies located outside the U.S.
- **Global stock funds** split their money between stocks of

foreign *and* domestic companies.
- **Corporate and government bond funds** seek a high level of current income by investing in corporate and/or government bonds. They are more conservative than stock funds and are geared toward income-oriented investors.
- **High-yield bond funds** (or junk bond funds) invest a high percentage of their portfolios in lower-rated bonds, which are riskier and, therefore, pay a higher rate of interest. Fund managers attempt to minimize risk through diversification, but high-yield bond funds are higher risk than many other types of funds and should make up at most only a small portion of your investment portfolio.
- **Sector funds** invest in one particular part of the economy, such as transportation, energy or biotechnology.

For more information about mutual funds:
- *Morningstar Mutual Funds* ($425 per year; 800–876–5005), a bi-monthly newsletter, offers a wealth of information about individual funds, including analysts' evaluations, and articles on how to choose and use them. The publication tracks more than 1,500 funds. *Morningstar Ascent* software ($95 for one year with quarterly updates; $195 for monthly updates) allows you to search and rank more than 7,300 funds and contains 15 years of historical data. It also lets you print out a one-page summary for each fund. Morningstar products and limited amounts of fund data are also available through America Online at the "Morningstar Marketplace."
- Value Line made a name for itself with its stock reports, but now offers mutual fund information as well. *Value Line Investment Survey* ($570 per year; 800–535–9648 ext. 2730) follows more than 1,700 stocks in its bi-monthly newsletters, providing almost every bit of data an investor could want, plus analysts' evaluations. *Value Line Mutual Funds* ($295 per year) offers the same type of information about 1,500 mutual funds in a similar format.
- *No-Load Fund Analyst* ($225 per year; 510–254–9017) tracks more than 100 funds that don't levy sales charges in its monthly reports—each covers six to eight funds.

Lots of useful data plus helpful articles and analyses of investment markets.
- *Alexander Steele's Mutual Fund Expert* software ($45 for a single installment, $95 for four quarterly installments or $185 for 12 monthly installments; 800–237–8400) lets you sort, rank and compare more than 8,700 mutual funds using a slew of performance, fee and management information provided on disk. You can get new data monthly, quarterly or whenever you choose for the prices listed above.

Because these references are so expensive to own, you may want to look for them in a local university library or a large regional or metropolitan library. Some brokerage offices also carry them. For more affordable help, a number of newsstand periodicals offer articles and performance data to help you choose and use stocks, bonds and funds. *Kiplinger's Personal Finance Magazine* provides in-depth fund analysis in its March and September issues as well as year-round articles and updates, and investment information is also available in *Money, Smart Money, The Wall Street Journal, Investors Business Daily* and *Barron's*.

If you'd rather browse the Internet, the following websites offer a lot of information for investors. To save time, the Kiplinger home page (www.kiplinger.com) provides a hypertext link to each of these sites:
- *CNNfn* (www.cnnfn.com) gives you a review of the day's business and investment news, a personal-finance feature section called "Your Money" and access to lots of information about major companies. Guest experts answer e-mail questions.
- *INVESTools* (www.investools.com) offers a selection of more than 30 financial newsletters and publications you can buy piecemeal. You can gather information about a company by entering the name or symbol. *Morningstar Mutual Fund Reports*, for example, are available for $5 each.
- *Mutual Funds Interactive* (www.brill.com) gives you experts' commentary on funds plus fund manager profiles, fund investing basics, and links to fund home pages and other fund-related websites.

- *NETworth* (networth.galt.com) lets you search for the 25 best-performing mutual funds by category or time period and then link to their *Morningstar* reports. Or you can search a database of 200 funds by total return, sales fees and other criteria. You can also access fund home pages and link to home pages for nearly 1,800 public companies.

Real Estate

Although some people are able to do well buying and selling investment real estate or acting as landlords over several pieces of rental property, the easiest way to add a real estate component to your portfolio is with real estate investment trusts (REITs). *Equity REITs* (rhymes with eats) are the most popular type. They are pools of income-producing property that are traded on the major stock exchanges. As a shareholder, you own a stake in the properties, which can include apartment buildings, shopping centers, office buildings and hotels, and receive regular income that is derived from rents. Thus you can invest in big commercial real estate deals with relatively small amounts of money. And because shares are bought and sold every day on the exchanges, they're easy to acquire and get rid of. But, like any stock, they are subject to the gyrations of the stock market.

REITs tend to pay high yields and involve a high level of risk. Look for REITs that own property in areas with strong growth potential, such as the Southwestern and Southeastern states, and that have relatively low levels of debt. Also, check the payout ratio (dividends paid divided by cash flow). A low payout ratio means a REIT can probably sustain its current dividend rate even if cash-flow growth slows. Compare a REIT's current payout ratio to past payouts and to those of its peers. Apartment REITs average 82%; neighborhood shopping REITs, 84%.

Since most REITs focus on one type of property or on a certain region of the country, you can lessen your risk by investing in a couple of different types that are invested in different areas. Or, for one-step diversification, consider a REIT mutual fund—they usually have "real estate" or "realty" in their names.

Allocating Your Assets

One factor that has a major effect on the performance of your investment portfolio is how your assets are divided among stocks, fixed-income investments and cash equivalents, such as money-market funds. Yet many investors spend very little time thinking about whether their asset allocation is appropriate. Several times in this section we've referred to the concept of diversification. This is the "don't-put-all-your-eggs-in-one-basket" philosophy of investing—the idea being that the more types of investments you own, the less your portfolio will be hurt when one market takes a dive or one type of investing falls out of favor.

The key to diversification is owning investments that perform differently under the same economic conditions. That way, no matter what's going on with the markets, part of your portfolio will still be making money. That also means that in a properly diversified portfolio, a few investments will probably be losing money at any given time.

The first step in evaluating how well your investment portfolio is diversified is to collect a recent statement on each investment and tally up the total you have allocated to stocks or stock mutual funds, bonds and other fixed-income investments, and cash or cash equivalents. Once you know how much money you have in each category, add them up and calculate what percentage of your money is in each category. For example, say you have $50,000 in investments and $25,000 of it is in individual stocks and stock funds, $15,000 of it is in bonds and GICs (Guaranteed Investment Contracts) and $10,000 of it is in a money-market fund. Your asset allocation is 50% stocks, 30% fixed income and 20% cash.

The second step in assessing your portfolio's asset allocation is determining what allocation is appropriate for your situation and goals. If you read a number of financial publications, you've probably seen conflicting advice on how your portfolio should be allocated while you're saving for retirement. That's because there is no one right answer that suits everyone. Model portfolios, such as the ones suggested on the following pages, may not meet your needs precisely, even if they're designed for people in your stage of life. Reason: Your asset allocation must take into account not only your age, but also the amount of money you have to invest and your tolerance for risk. Instead of making changes in your holdings every time you see a new suggestion, use model portfolios as general guidelines for how you should be invested and to help make adjustments as you go along. You also might want to meet with a professional at least once as you near retirement to make sure your asset allocation will meet your needs and long-term goals. (See page 69 for help with finding a financial adviser.) Here are some suggested portfolio mixes for people in their forties, fifties and sixties who are saving and investing for retirement:

- **People in their 40s.** This is a go-for-growth portfolio suited for people who are still two decades or more from retirement. They can afford a higher-risk mix of investments than someone who is about to start drawing income from their portfolio.

  The need for a cash allocation will vary depending upon whether they have some way to get money quickly when unexpected expenses arise. For example, if there's a home equity line of credit that they can draw on, the cash portion of the portfolio can be eliminated and the money can be invested in fixed-income instead.

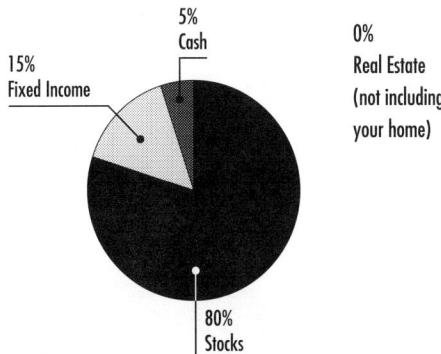

5% Cash
15% Fixed Income
0% Real Estate (not including your home)
80% Stocks

- **People in Their 50s.** As you move into your 50s, there are subtle but important shifts to make. You'll want to be a bit more conservative and, since you'll have more money in your portfolio, you'll be able to diversify further by adding

REITs. Your overall breakdown doesn't need to change that much, but you'll want to add some income stocks to the stock portion and maybe shift some of your bond investments from long-term to intermediate term.

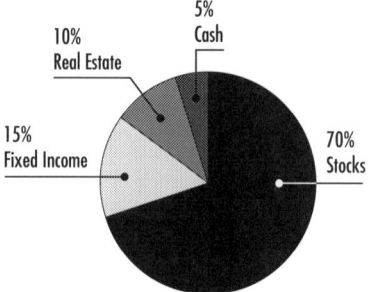

- **People in Their 60s.** When you're less than 10 years from retirement, there's a tendency to become super-conservative. The shortening time frame does call for a more conservative approach, but you still need to stay well-diversified. If all your money is in fixed-income investments, the income from those assets will not grow over the years and will, in fact, lose value as inflation eats away at it. To lessen the risk you're taking with the stock portion of your portfolio somewhat, blue chip and income stocks should dominate those holdings.

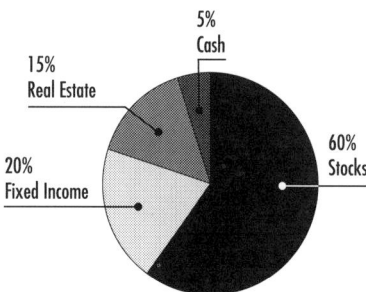

After you've determined the appropriate portfolio allocation for your situation and risk tolerance, you need to follow its progress to make sure it will achieve your goals. For some that means using the newspaper or a computer to check on their holdings every day, or even several times a day. That's probably not necessary and may even be a bad idea if watching every rise and dip in the markets makes you queasy and prompts a lot of premature buying and selling.

The shifts in allocations that are indicated by the preceding piecharts are the big changes you'll make over time. But in between, you'll want to make smaller changes that will keep your portfolio in line with the asset allocation you've chosen. Most professionals advise reviewing your entire portfolio once every quarter, or at least once a year. Look at the portfolio as a whole to make sure that big gains or losses in one type of investment haven't skewed your original allocation. Go over each investment to make sure it's performing in line with, or better than, the average or index for that type of investment. If not, determine why and whether the cause warrants reducing your holding or selling it altogether.

Shifting your money around too much can hurt your bottom line, because of the tax bills that the selling might generate. You also need to keep an eye on the commissions or loads you'll pay for doing too much buying and selling. For those reasons, consider using the "annual or 10%" rule. That means you review your portfolio regularly, but make changes only annually or when your asset allocation deviates by 10% or more, whichever comes first.

Using a Financial Adviser

With this guidebook, you're putting together a plan for a successful retirement, but you could probably benefit from sitting down with a professional when it comes time to work out the details. You may already have a trusted adviser, broker or banker who helps you with your investment selections. But it can be well worth the money to have a financial planner review your entire financial picture as you prepare for retirement, and perhaps to do periodic checks on your progress as well.

Start your search by getting referrals from friends, relatives and professionals you deal with already, but avoid hiring close friends or relatives—holding them responsible for the advice they give could damage your relationship. Don't hire someone until you've checked him or her thoroughly and talked enough to get an idea of the kind of help he or she will provide; if you lack confidence in the adviser's knowledge and judgment, you're not likely to act on the advice. That's a sure waste of time and money.

Investigate the Firm

Call each financial adviser and ask for a description of his or her services, charges and investment philosophy. Also, ask for a copy of form ADV, Part II, which advisers are required to file with the Securities and Exchange Commission when they register as an investment adviser. The form lists the educational and business backgrounds of key individuals, such as the firm's owners. (If the ADV doesn't have the background of the person you are considering, ask for it.) You are entitled to a copy of the ADV II or another document—usually a brochure—setting out the same information. The exception is that an adviser can withhold the ADV II until a contract is signed, but you have five days to end the agreement without paying a penalty. Don't hire anyone who isn't registered as an investment adviser with the SEC, or doesn't work for a firm registered as an adviser, and who isn't willing to give you ADV II before you sign on.

Understand the Fee Structure

ADV II shows how the practitioner gets paid: with a fee, by commission or some combination of fee and commission.

- ***Fee-only advisers*** typically charge a flat fee or hourly rates, or a percentage of the assets a client gives them to manage. They don't earn commissions for selling financial products to you.
- ***Commission-based advisers*** earn their money by selling stocks, bonds, mutual funds, life insurance and the like—usually to implement a financial plan drawn up in consultation with them.
- ***Fee-and-commission-based advisers*** typically charge a straight fee for advice or for drawing up a financial plan. Then, during what is often called the implementation phase, you will pay a commission for financial products

you buy or pay an annual fee for assets under management. Advisers who work for a management fee usually require at least $100,000 in assets.

Watch for Conflicts of Interest

Commission-based and fee-and-commission-based registered advisers have to disclose how they are paid, but they don't have to explain that they may be tempted to recommend investments that will pay the biggest commissions.

Check for Disciplinary Actions

Next, check with your state's securities regulator. Most states regulate investment advisers and provide access to information in the Central Registration Depository (CRD), operated jointly by state regulators and the National Association of Securities Dealers. Steer clear of anyone with a checkered disciplinary history or who isn't registered. (If you can't find the phone number of your regulator, get it from the North American Securities Administrators Association, 202–737–0900.)

Look at Credentials

By itself, the term financial planner or adviser means little. Many brokers whose income depends solely on commissions from stocks, bonds and mutual funds with sales loads routinely call themselves financial planners. Look for designations and credentials that, when paired with years of full-time experience and solid recommendations, are evidence of a good planner. For example, a CFP (Certified Financial Planner) designation requires three years of work experience, two years of course work and a passing score on a five-part exam.

Visit Finalists at Their Offices

The first half-hour or so should be free. Make sure to get a copy of the contract you will be asked to sign. Will the adviser be willing to work with your lawyer or CPA? Are you comfortable talking with him or her? No matter how good the adviser, if the chemistry between you is bad, look elsewhere.

Chapter 9

Planning Your Pension Payout

Once you've got your investment portfolio in good shape, your next step is to look at how the money in your pension plan will be distributed to you at retirement—keeping in mind that if you are 10 or more years from retirement, you'll need to reexamine your pension situation when you're only five years from retiring because the plan may be altered in the meantime.

Depending on what type of pension or pensions you have, you may have a lot of decision-making to do at retirement. With many defined-benefit plans, you have no choice other than receiving the pension in the form of monthly payments. But you may have to choose between a number of annuity options that can make a significant difference in how much you receive. With defined-contribution plans, you have the choice of taking your money in a lump sum and paying taxes on it or rolling it over into an IRA. Some defined-benefit plans also offer these choices.

The more you know about these options, the better off you'll be when the time comes to make your decision. You can't take this too seriously because once you've made your choice, you cannot change your mind.

Annuity Options

The guaranteed monthly payment from your defined-benefit plan can be provided by a single-life annuity—payments will stop when you die. If you're single and have no one to provide for, that's the best choice and will give you the largest benefit. But you'll want to consider other annuity options if your survivors will need the benefits after you're gone. The annuity payout options you're likely to have were explained on page 33.

If you're married, you must take a 50% joint and survivor (J&S) annuity, unless your spouse puts it in writing that it's okay for you to pick another option. The 50% option guarantees that the survivor will keep getting half the benefit after the other beneficiary dies. There are some other annuity options you should consider if you fit one of the following descriptions.

You're Short on Savings

If you and your spouse will be depending on your pension and social security for most of your retirement income, your best choice will be a J&S annuity with the 75% or 100% option, rather than the standard 50% J&S annuity. When retirement resources are limited, it's often hard for a surviving spouse to get along when pension income drops by more than 25%. With the 100% option, there's no drop in check size after one dies. But the security of a 100% J&S option is expensive: Since the benefits will be spread out over both your lifetime and your spouse's, your monthly benefit will be 20% to 25% less than it would have been with a single-life annuity, which would pay out only while you live.

You Have Plenty of Money

You're all set for retirement, perhaps because of a big 401(k) payout. When a defined-benefit pension is a smaller part of your total retirement income, the single-life or 50% J&S options are good choices for you. A 50% J&S annuity provides a monthly benefit that's about 10% to 20% smaller than a single-life annuity.

Both Spouses Have Pensions

In this instance, it's sometimes best for each to choose a single-life annuity, if both spouses have generous pensions.

This will maximize pension income while both are alive and ensure income for the survivor after one dies. However, if one pension benefit is significantly larger than the other, a J&S option should be considered on the larger one to protect the spouse with the smaller benefit.

You're Retiring Early

You will have to wait a few years before your social security checks start coming so check to see if your employer's plan offers a level-income or social security equalization option. This starts you off with a higher benefit that drops when social security kicks in.

Your Health Is Poor

If the odds favor your spouse outliving you by many years, look hard at the 100% J&S option. If you're single and you have heirs you'd like to help out, think about an option called "life with ten- or 20-years certain." Ten-years certain means payments will continue for at least ten years, even if you die before that term is up. The payouts after your death would go to the designated beneficiary. That option is likely to cost you a 7% reduction in benefits. 20-years certain—with a guaranteed payment period of 20 years—will mean about an 18% cut.

You'll Probably Outlive Your Spouse

Here a single-life annuity is probably best. There's not much sense in opting for a smaller check to buy coverage for a partner who isn't likely to survive you. If you want to provide some protection for your spouse just in case, go with the 50% J&S. Some plans offer an option known as "pension max." The pensioner takes a single-life annuity and uses the "extra" income from this option to purchase life insurance to assure the beneficiary of an income stream. Do some careful number crunching before you buy into this kind of plan, especially if you're close to the normal retirement age. The older you are, the higher the cost of the life insurance. And the more the insurance costs, the less likely it is the plan will work in your favor. If your employer offers a number of J&S options, one of those is usually a better deal.

IRA Rollovers

With a defined-contribution plan—and when the option is available on a defined-benefit plan—rolling your pension money directly into an IRA is probably the most sensible solution. While you could take the money in a lump-sum payout, you'll run into tax issues that require special considerations, as explained on page 76. The shelter of an IRA allows the earnings on the principal to go untaxed until withdrawn. This can be quite beneficial, especially if you don't plan to take any money from the IRA for a while. For example, say you rollover $400,000 into an IRA earning 8% a year and make no withdrawals. Allowed to grow tax free, this IRA would swell to about $587,000 after five years and $863,000 after ten.

The key, as explained on page 6, is to arrange to have your employer make a *direct* rollover from the pension plan to the IRA. If you do a hands-on rollover—withdrawing the money from the plan and depositing it in an IRA within 60 days—you will ultimately avoid paying income taxes on the money. But in the short run, you'll be hit with a 20% withholding tax when you take it out and you'll have to replace that 20% when you deposit the sum in the IRA in order for it to qualify as a rollover. (At tax time, you can apply to get it back as a tax refund.) One thing to note about this is that you won't be able to rollover any after-tax contributions you made to your pension plan. After-tax contributions can be withdrawn tax free with no penalty at retirement.

If you have the option of doing a rollover and you prefer the security of lifetime payouts that an annuity provides, it's possible to roll your money directly into a deferred annuity. That continues the tax deferral on the money because none will be due until you "annuitize"—start receiving regular payouts from the annuity.

Lump-Sum Payouts

If you decide to cash out of your plan by taking a lump-sum payout instead of rolling the money into an IRA, the worst thing you can do is spend it. Maybe you plan to pay off your mortgage, buy a new home for retirement or start a small business with the money. That may work for some people who have plenty of other assets to live on in retirement, but for most people it's a bad idea. Remember, that lump sum is your pension and should be set aside and invested to do what it is intended to do: Provide income that you can live on throughout retirement.

When you choose a lump-sum payout, you'll owe income taxes on the money. However, if you were born before 1936 or plan to retire before the year 2000, you may be able to lessen the blow by using something called *five- or ten-year averaging*. Basically, these computations tax the distribution all at once, but the bill is figured as though you received the money over a number of years. Although you must actually pay the tax right away, the amount due will be significantly less than if the full amount was heaped on top of your other taxable income.

Congress replaced ten-year averaging with the five-year method in 1986 and then, in 1996, repealed five-year averaging on lump-sum distributions received after 1999. If you were born before 1936, you can still use the ten-year method. If not, you're left with the five-year method, but only if you'll be receiving your lump sum by the end of 1999. Anyone retiring after 1999 and choosing a lump-sum payout will have to pay the full tax on the lump sum for the year it's received. This change makes a lump-sum distribution a pretty bad choice for future retirees.

If your age means you will qualify for either five- or ten-year averaging, figuring out which produces the best result for you is a complicated undertaking and should be done with the help of an accountant or tax lawyer. Here's how five-year averaging works: Divide your distribution by 5. Find the tax on that amount using the current rates for single taxpayers (your actual filing status and any other income you have for the year don't matter for this calculation). Multiply that tax by 5 to calculate the total tax bill on your lump sum.

For ten-year averaging, you divide the distribution by 10 and then multiply the one-year tax amount by 10. Ten-year averaging, however, requires that you use 1986 tax rates, which are considerably higher than current rates.

After you pay the tax calculated with averaging, there's no further federal tax liability on the money. But in order to qualify to use either type of averaging, your lump sum must:
- be paid out after age 59½;
- come from a qualified plan you participated in for at least five years before the distribution is made;
- represent your entire interest in the plan and be paid to you within a single tax year; and
- be paid to you after you leave the job or, if you continue working, after the plan's retirement age.

Making Your Choice

To aid you in making the right choice for your situation, the table on the next page breaks out some of the pros and cons involved with each of the options you may have to consider.

Once those points have helped you start thinking about the big issues involved in the decision, it's a good idea to sit down with a professional adviser—an accountant, a financial planner or someone in your company's benefits department—and work out which option is likely to produce the most income after taxes, taking into account your and your family's needs and your tolerance for risk.

Another point to keep in mind: A major advantage of rolling the money into an IRA or taking a lump sum is that it becomes part of your estate. If, for example, you or your spouse died soon after choosing an annuity option offered by your company, your heirs wouldn't necessarily collect a dime. But if the money were in a rollover IRA, the money could go to your heirs as part of your estate. (For more on estate planning, see page 125.)

Pension-Payout Options

Company-purchased annuity

Advantages	**Disadvantages**
You get a safe, steady stream of income for life.	You can't get your money in case you need a big chunk of it.
You can provide survivor's benefits for your spouse.	You forfeit a chance to use favorable tax treatments.
There's no big tax bite all at once.	Die prematurely and you would lose all or part of your pension, if you chose a single-life annuity without death benefits.

IRA rollovers

Advantages	**Disadvantages**
Tax deferred until withdrawal.	Withdrawals taxed as ordinary income. No special tax treatment when you take the money out.
Tax-deferred compounding.	
	Withdrawals prior to age 59½ are penalized.

Taxable lump sum

Advantages	**Disadvantages**
You have immediate access to your money.	Current taxation.
The funds are yours and pass to your heirs at death.	You lose earning power compared with an IRA rollover because the money you pay in taxes can't earn interest or dividends.
Potential favorable tax treatment, if you qualify for ten-year averaging or will receive your lump sum by the end of 1999 and can use the five-year method.	Risk of spending down your retirement nest egg too soon.

Chapter 10

Tapping the Money in Your Home

The home you've lived in, played in, worked on and paid for over the last several years is probably one of your most valuable assets. It can play an important role in your retirement planning. If you're well on your way to paying off your mortgage and you're happy with the house's location, you might be thinking about continuing to live in that house in retirement. Once it's paid for, not having to spend a big chunk of money on housing every month will mean that you won't need as much income in retirement—or that you can enjoy spending the income you do have on travel, sports, hobbies or whatever it is you like to do. Or maybe you plan to sell your house and use part of the proceeds to buy a smaller, more manageable home in a less expensive area or a warmer climate, adding the rest of the money from the sale to your nest egg.

If you don't want to be saddled with the responsibilities of owning a home in retirement, selling your house could provide a chunk of money that you can invest and draw on to pay rent on a place where someone else mows the lawn and watches the property, leaving you free to come and go as you please.

Whether you decide to stay or you choose to sell, the following suggestions can help you get the most financial benefit from the house in which you've invested so much time and money.

Tax Advantages of Selling Your Home

Prior to the Taxpayer's Relief Act of 1997, if you owned more than one home over the years, you probably rolled the profit from one house into the next, delaying the tax bill as you worked your way up to the more expensive home you live in now. You may have only vaguely wondered when the IRS was going to make its move and claim those unpaid taxes. If you decided to sell your home and rent or buy a less expensive home, it would then be time to pay the piper. The good news was that if you or your spouse were age 55 or older you'd probably qualify for a one-time tax break that allowed you to escape the capital gains tax on up to $125,000 of profit from the sale of your home.

Thanks to the 1997 law, your home can now be an even bigger contributor to your retirement plans. Congress abolished the $125,000 exclusion rule and replaced it with one that lets you take up to $250,000 of home-sale profit tax-free for those who file single returns and up to $500,000 if you file a joint return. There's no age requirement for this break and you can use it over and over again, as long as you don't use it more than once in any two-year period.

To qualify for the break, you must have owned and lived in the home for at least two of the five years leading up to the sale. There's an exception to the rule if poor health or a job-related move leads to the sale.

What If Your Home Doesn't Sell?

You may want to consider turning it into a rental property. But there's a potential catch to converting: The value of the house for figuring depreciation deductions—a key write-off for real estate investors—is your adjusted basis or the fair market value of the house, whichever is less. The basis may be far less than what the house is worth when you start renting it, particularly if you have lowered the basis by rolling over profit from previous homes.

Another factor to consider is that the tax-free profit rules apply only to your principal residence. Can a house that's being rented when you finally sell it qualify as your home?

The good news is that it can, if you can show that the rental was temporary. There's no hard and fast rule for how long a "temporary" rental can last before it becomes permanent, but clearly, the longer the rental, the more evidence you'll need showing that you were really trying to sell it. Also, to qualify for the tax-free profit, you'll have to sell within three years of the time you move out—so you still pass the two-out-of-five-year residency test.

Another alternative that you may have to consider is selling your home for a loss. But keep in mind that losses from home sales are not deductible. You may have heard that you can deduct a home-sale loss if, prior to the sale, you convert the house to a rental property. But there's a catch that makes this tactic worthless. The basis for figuring your loss begins as the lower of the adjusted basis or fair market value at the time of the conversion to a rental. (The basis is increased for any improvements after the conversion and reduced for any depreciation claimed.) In other words, any loss in fair market value that occurs while you're living in the house still can't be deducted.

Second Homes That Become Retirement Homes

Many people also think about buying a second home while they are still working and then renting it out until they're ready to retire and move there. This is a good idea from the point of view that while it's a rental property, you can deduct your expenses including mortgage interest, property taxes, operating costs and depreciation up to the amount of your rental income. (Excess expenses would be subject to the passive-loss rules.)

If you have a vacation home that you don't rent out, you can legally squeeze tax-free profit out of it. After you sell what has been your principal residence and cash in on up to $500,000 of tax-free profit, move into the vacation place and make it your new principal residence for at least two years. As soon as you meet the two-years-out-of-five residency requirement, you can sell that home and the profit, again up to $500,000 qualifies for tax-free treatment.

If you do rent out the vacation house, the profit wouldn't

be 100% tax-free, but you could still have additional money from the sale to feather your retirement nest.

Pros and Cons of Reverse Mortgages

For many people who manage to pay off their mortgage before they retire, staying put sounds very appealing. They like the idea of a retirement free of mortgage or rent payments, and look forward to continuing to live in a familiar area where they'll be close to family and old friends. But there may come a time when the need for more income makes having so much money tied up in the house seem impractical—even if they love the house and would like to pass it on to their children. That's when a reverse mortgage (RM) can make sense. However, these products are complicated and aren't appropriate for everyone, so consider this option carefully.

With a reverse mortgage, a lender allows you to borrow a portion of the equity in your home while you continue living in it. You don't have to pay back what you borrow until the home is sold—either when you move or after you die. Since you're not actually selling the home yet, there are no tax consequences, and the money you get from the RM is tax free.

RMs are usually available only to homeowners who are age 62 or older. How much you can borrow depends on your life expectancy and how much equity the lender will take into account for the loan. Because the amount you can draw out is determined partly by your life expectancy, the older you are, the higher the payments you can get from a given amount of equity.

Depending on the RM you choose, you can convert your home equity into an income stream, a lump sum, a line of credit or some combination. A line of credit is the most popular choice because of the flexibility it allows. When comparing RMs, lenders are required to provide you with the total annual loan cost (or TALC) rates on the various loans. The TALC rate takes into account all charges associated with the loan, including interest, closing costs, mortgage insurance and servicing fees, and the cost of any annuity you buy as part of the RM transaction. When comparing lines of credit, look closely at the numbers. The total amount of cash you can access immediately, and over time, can vary by thousands of dollars.

The most popular type of RMs are federally insured Home Equity Conversion Mortgages, or HECMs, from the Federal Housing Administration (FHA). The insurance program protects you if your lender defaults. These loans are available everywhere except South Dakota and Texas. The FHA sets a limit on the amount you can borrow, which is partially based on the median home value in your area, no matter how much your home is actually worth. That limit varies depending on where you live. But in the highest-cost areas (not including Alaska and Hawaii), the current limit is $155,250.

For more information and a state-by-state list of lenders' phone numbers, order Your New Retirement Nest Egg: A Consumer Guide to the New Reverse Mortgages ($24.95 plus $4.50 shipping) from the National Center for Home Equity Conversion (Suite 115, 7373 147th St. West, Apple Valley, MN 55124; 800–247–6553). Also, the American Association of Retired Persons (AARP) offers a free "Home Equity Conversion Kit." Send a request, including the kit's stock number (D15601), to AARP Fulfillment, 601 E Street, N.W., Washington, DC 20049.

Using a Sale-leaseback

A sale-leaseback is another option for people who want to stay in their current home, but need to generate some income from it.

Sale-leasebacks work like this: You sell your house to one of your adult children, who leases it back to you for the rest of your life. The buyer generally puts up a 10% to 20% down payment and pays all property taxes, insurance and maintenance. You pay rent to the buyer. The buyer gets a mortgage on the home and pays you a lump sum with which you can buy an annuity that provides a steady income. Or you can play banker by accepting a 10% or 20% down payment, lending the buyer the difference and collecting monthly payments, from which you pay the rent. Either way, you get to continue living in your home and get access to the equity you've built up in it.

Once again, profit on the sale of $250,000 reported on single returns or $500,000 on joint returns is tax-free.

The National Center for Home Equity Conversion offers a publication called Sale-Leaseback Guide and Model Documents ($39 postpaid), which provides legal and financial guidance on structuring sale-leaseback transactions. The model documents may have to be adapted in states where land contracts rather than deeds of trust are the norm.

If you decide to work out this kind of transaction with one of your children, be sure the deal makes financial sense or the IRS may disallow it. The major problem area is rent; it must be set reasonably close to the market rate for the location. To be safe, have a lawyer help you arrange it.

P A R T   4

Making Lifestyle Decisions

Although the financial side of planning your retirement is absolutely crucial, making decisions about where you'll live and how you'll spend your time is also important—and a lot more fun! Too often people figure they'll work out these kinds of plans after they're retired, when they'll have more time to think about it. But experts find you'll be more likely to be satisfied in retirement if you start planning where you will live and what you will do beforehand. And, of course, the cost of living where you decide to spend your retirement will have an effect on how much money you'll need.

Think about whether you want to continue working part-time after you retire. Vacation in the places where you might want to live or spend part of your time. Try out some of the different types of volunteering or hobbies that you hope to get involved in when you're retired. The following chapters offer suggestions and resources to get you started.

Chapter 11

Working in Retirement

Retirement has become somewhat of a misnomer as more people feel that they are too young and energetic at 65 to settle into a life of leisure. Many find that they need additional income to fund what may be a 30-year retirement. Others, seeking to remain active, volunteer their time, as discussed in Chapter 13. According to the Bureau of Labor Statistics, about 12% of people age 65 and older are currently part of the civilian labor force and 30% of people 55 and older are working.

Some "retirees" use their skills and experience to land a job in a whole new field, while others work part-time or act as a consultant for their old employer. Those with entrepreneurial spirit may choose to start their own small businesses. Some are unsure about what they want to do next and head back to school to see where that leads them.

If you think work will be part of your retirement plan, either by necessity or by choice, start planning for that well in advance of when you leave your current job.

Finding Your Second Career

Some retirement experts are finding that people who assume they will be able to do some kind of full- or part-time work in retirement are often surprised at how difficult it is to find a job. In fact, a recent report from The Commonwealth Fund found that 12% of Americans age 55 and older are willing and able to work, but cannot find jobs. That won't be you, though, because you're taking the first step toward planning your post-retirement work now by reading this section.

If you want to try something new in retirement, but have no idea what kind of work you want to do, do some research and soul-searching before you start job-hunting. Start by taking one of the popular aptitude or personality tests that people use to learn more about what type of work fits their strengths and weaknesses. Talk with your family and friends about what activities they perceive you to enjoy the most or what type of work they think you might enjoy.

Here are some ways to find the new job or career that meets your needs:

- ***Check with your former employer.*** Your old company may be willing to rehire retirees on a part-time or consulting basis. Some large companies even have in-house job banks to match retirees with temporary work. Or you may be able to ease into retirement by switching to a shorter work week for several years before you actually retire. This will allow you to continue working in familiar surroundings with people you already know. But before you reduce your hours, make sure this won't have a negative impact on your pension benefits (page 9).

- ***Use an executive search firm.*** Send a cover letter and resume to Senior Careers Executive Search (257 Park Avenue South, New York, NY 10010; or fax to 212–228–3958, attn: Senior Careers). The firm, which is a division of the National Executive Service Corps (page 108), conducts searches for executives to fill jobs in nonprofit organizations. It matches executives with full- or part-time positions, as well as with some temporary consulting assignments. Most of the positions are in middle to upper management.

- ***Try temping.*** Some temporary agencies actively recruit older workers for a variety of positions, and temporary work may be the ideal choice if you want flexible hours. Kelly Services, for example, has a special program for workers 55 and older and has some 1,000 offices worldwide.

- **Get free help.** A free government help line called Eldercare Locator (800-677-1116) can tell you if there are any job placement agencies for older workers in your area.

The following books and resources may also help you decide what type of work you want to do in retirement:
- *What Color Is Your Parachute?* by Richard Nelson Bolles ($14.95; Ten Speed Press. Updated annually.)
- *Do What You Love, The Money Will Follow*, by Marsha Sinetar ($11.95; Dell Publishing).
- *Kiplinger's Retire & Thrive*, by Robert K. Otterbourg ($15 plus $3.50 shipping and handling; Kiplinger Books, 800-280-7165).
- *Finding Your Perfect Work*, by Paul and Sarah Edwards ($16.95; The Putnam Publishing Group).

Starting Your Own Business

Many people like the idea of working for themselves in retirement. They plan to try out business ideas that have been formulating in the back of their minds for some time. Some see this as a way to set their own hours and work at the pace they choose. But in reality, launching a successful small business usually involves working harder than they've ever worked before.

One key to success is research. Don't spend a lot of money seeing if your idea will work; find out as much as you can about the line of business you want to get into by researching your market thoroughly. A recent study shows that the average small business takes over two years in the planning stage.

Once you have a detailed plan, invest only as much money as you can afford to lose. Betting your whole nest egg on a business venture that doesn't work could leave you with almost nothing to live on in retirement.

Two popular ways to start a small business in retirement are hanging out a shingle and becoming a consultant and buying into a franchise operation. Here's a brief rundown of what you need to know if one of those approaches appeals to you.

Getting Started in Consulting

Some retirees turn to consulting as a way to be their own boss while continuing to work in their field. However, consulting is an extremely competitive business that requires planning and hard work. There's a lot to do before you order your first set of business cards.

- ***Identify a problem that's common in your field*** and determine how you can use your skills and experience to help companies or people solve it. Some examples: helping companies communicate better with writing, public speaking or advertising; improving office efficiency; or providing research support.
- ***Decide who will be your target market*** by doing some research to determine who needs the service you can provide. Find out what types of businesses and which territory you should target.
- ***Create a business plan*** that spells out what you're going to do and what you want to accomplish. Address such things as the purpose of your business, the service you will provide, your market and a projection of expenses and income. You'll probably also need a marketing plan, since creating interest in the service you provide and attracting clients are keys to success.
- ***Test the waters by calling on some potential clients***—contacts you have in the business, maybe your former employer—and trying out your idea. This can give you some sense of whether your service will sell.

Buying into a Franchise

A franchise offers the freedom and challenge of being your own boss but reduces your risk of failure because you have an established product or service to market, and the resources and support of the franchisor. To succeed, you'll need a substantial sum of money to invest and a willingness to work hard in an environment that's probably very different from the setting you may be used to.

There are franchising opportunities to suit any interest, including business services (accounting, tax preparation, executive recruiting), travel agencies, automotive care, public relations or home furnishings retail. Not all franchisors require experience in their specialty. Some just want general management experience or good business and people skills.

Typically you pay a franchise fee, royalties and other start-up expenses—and continuing costs as you go along—in exchange for a business formula, marketing image, training and other support services. Good franchise companies will provide a specific breakdown of what you can expect to spend. Successful, well-known franchises are the most expensive, but also the safer bet.

When choosing a franchise company, start by asking these questions: How long has the franchisor been in business? Is the company in good financial condition? (Full financial disclosure is required by the Federal Trade Commission.) How many franchises have been established and how many are in your area?

Some franchisor companies have started offering their products outside the franchises and, in some cases, cutting into franchisees' business. Find out if the company also sells through kiosks, carts and other scaled-down operations in airports, hospitals, schools or other stores in your area. Ask if the company does telemarketing, sells direct from its warehouses or offers products on the Internet.

Once you've narrowed down your choices, get the company's uniform operating circular or a disclosure statement that lists names, addresses and phone numbers of current and former franchisees. Contact a few of them and ask what their experience has been; find out if their costs were in line with the company's breakdown and if the franchisor has held up its end of the deal.

No matter what type of small business you're interested in running, you'll benefit from getting all the advice you can from people who already own their own successful business.

In addition to talking to business owners you know, these books and resources offer a lot of helpful information:

- Service Corps of Retired Executives (SCORE) has 389 chapters around the country, which provide free counseling and mentoring services to budding entrepreneurs. The volunteer counselors are retired professionals who have a lot of business experience to share.

  SCORE also conducts workshops and seminars on starting a business that cost around $20 to $50. Call 800–634–0245 to locate the chapter nearest you. You can also contact SCORE through the Small Business Association's website at www.sba.gov.

- *100 Best Retirement Businesses*, by Lisa Angowski Rogak ($15.95 plus $5 shipping and handling; Upstart Publishing, 800–235–8866).

- *How to Succeed as an Independent Consultant*, by Herman Holtz ($29.95; John Wiley & Sons).

- The International Franchise Association (P.O. Box 1020, Sewickley, PA 15143; 800–543–1038) offers the *Franchise Opportunities Guide* ($15 plus $6 shipping on an order of up to three of IFA's books), which lists about 3,000 franchise companies, contact information, franchisee qualifications and estimated investment. IFA also offers a booklet called *Investigate Before Investing* ($6) and a number of other books and brochures on getting financing, evaluating the information from the franchise company and more. Plus, the IFA conducts workshops and expos around the country. The sessions are a good way to meet franchisees and find out about their experiences. Call 202–628–8000 and ask for the conferences department to order a calendar of events.

- *Kiplinger's Working for Yourself: Full Time, Part Time, Anytime*, by Joseph Anthony ($15.00 plus $3.50 shipping and handling; Kiplinger Books, 800–280–7165).

- *Home Business Big Business: How To Launch Your Home Business and Make It a Success*, by Mel Cook ($12; MacMillan Publishing).

- *Tax Savvy for Small Business*, by Frederick W. Daily ($26.95; Nolo Press), and *How to Write a Business Plan*, by Mike McKeever ($21.95; Nolo Press).

Going Back to School

Maybe you didn't get the degree you wanted earlier in life because you couldn't afford it or you didn't have time. Perhaps you've come across a new and interesting field in the course of your career and want to get the master's degree you need to work in it. Or you may have no interest in taking courses for credit, but would like to audit courses to learn about something that interests you or add to your knowledge of a given field. For these reasons and more, middle-aged students are becoming a more familiar sight on college campuses around the country.

Start your search for the right program at the community colleges and four-year institutions in your area. Many state universities and colleges allow retirees who are state residents to audit regular undergraduate classes at little or no cost. For example, the University of South Carolina offers free auditing for people over 60 and the University of Nevada offers it to those over 62. The University of Washington charges people over 60 $5 per semester to audit a class.

If you'd rather not attend class with students who are much younger than you, there are several options for learning with people closer to your age.

Association of Graduate Liberal Arts

More than 100 colleges and universities belong to this program, which allows men and women over 30 to pursue nontraditional courses of study on a schedule that fits into their workweek. The curriculum in the Association's programs is interdisciplinary, allowing students to design their own course of study. However, the program is for people who are degree-oriented. Students are usually required to make a commitment to acquire a degree by attending the school for at least three years as a part-time student or one year for full-time students. No thesis is required, but students must submit an essay based on original research.

The tuition for the Association's programs varies depending on whether you're at a public or private university, but some students do qualify for financial aid. Call the registrar's office at local schools to find out if they offer an Association program, also known as Master of Arts in Liberal Studies (MALS) programs.

Learning-in-Retirement (LIR) Centers

LIR programs are available on more than 200 campuses across the country and have tens of thousands of members. While they all differ in design, they have several things in common: Members determine their own curriculum, teach their own courses and market and administer the program. The college or university provides the classroom space and some limited funding. Courses cover everything from art history to current events and from investing to Broadway musicals. Membership fees range around $150 to $250 a year.

LIR programs are available at the University of Delaware in Wilmington, the University of North Carolina in Asheville, Northwestern University in Evanston, Ill., Duke University in Durham, N.C., and at UCLA, just to name a few. To locate the LIR program nearest you, contact the Elderhostel Institute Network (56 Dover Road, Durham, NH 03824; 603–862–0725).

Go On-line

If you have a computer and access to America Online, CompuServe or the Internet, you can take your pick of dozens of credit and non-credit courses offered on-line. In some cases you can even register and pay for your class without picking up the phone or writing a check.

- ***America Online (AOL) offers the Electronic University Network (EUN).*** Once you're connected to AOL, select "education" from the main menu, then "EUN." The program offers undergraduate and graduate level courses from eight accredited colleges and universities. Course work usually involves one or more of the following: "real time" lectures in which students and teacher interact on-line; e-mail communications between you and your instructor; message boards where you can discuss ongoing class work with other enrolled students; and "libraries" to help with assignments. The cost is $59 to $300 per credit hour depending on the school, plus on-line time. To get a feel for what it's like, sign up for EUN's free minicourse. Send an e-mail message on AOL to EUNLearn, along with your real name, address, phone number, and type of college program that interests you. EUN also provides free software for a visit on-line. Call 800–225–3276 and leave your name and address. Specify whether you need DOS, Windows or Macintosh format.

Another AOL option, *Interactive Education Services*, offers continuing education courses. (The key word for getting to this area is "IES.") You could take a 6- to 8-week class on earth ethics, economics or creative writing, for example. Classes meet weekly for an hour or two, often at night. Your cost: $25 to $100, plus on-line time and whatever you spend on reading materials and on-line research.

Call 800–827–6364 for subscription prices to AOL.

- ***CompuServe's College and Adult Students Forum*** has lots of offerings. Once you're on CompuServe, pull down the "Services" menu, click on the "Go" option and type "stufob." That will take you straight to the forum with its own conference and chat rooms, message areas and libraries. For information on on-line courses and degrees available from dozens of colleges and universities, go to "Library" in the top menu. To join CompuServe, call 800–848–8199.
- ***The Internet*** offers the most extensive on-line class offerings. *Globewide Network Academy (GNA),* for example, is a consortium of educational and research organizations that offers on-line courses leading to degrees. GNA has a site on the World Wide Web, which lists over 400 courses in topics such as art, computers, language, literature and writing. For instructions on reaching the web server from America Online, Delphi or Prodigy, check the catalog at the Web's Uniform Resource Locator (URL), www.gnacademy.org. GNA's non-credit courses run from a few dollars up to $100, credit courses cost about $100 per credit hour. Neither fee includes on-line time.

Virtual Online University (VOU) is a nonprofit corporation offering professional, degree and continuing-education courses from Athena University. (Athena is a "virtual" university—it exists on-line but has no physical location, buildings or classrooms—and is working toward accreditation.) Students can pursue B.A. and M.A. degrees in liberal arts.

Continuing education courses run from 2 to 13 weeks, usually meeting for an hour or two a week on a "real time" interactive basis with the instructor. Credit courses, which typically take 13 weeks, cost about $100 per credit hour. Non-credit courses are priced according to length and the time it takes to teach. Neither fee includes on-line time. You can find out about VOU's classes, orientation sessions, registration and fees at its website (www.iac.net/~billp).

The Internet is accessible via America Online, CompuServe and Prodigy, but if you plan on taking classes or making extensive use of it, the cheapest access is probably through a regional Internet service provider.

Chapter 12

Where Will You Live?

You've decided you want to move when you retire. You probably have some idea of where you'd like to live—what part of the country, what size town or city, or what type of climate. Maybe you want to move to a quieter, more rural area where you can slow your pace down a bit. Or you want to live in a warmer climate or a place where there are more opportunities for outdoor recreation. Perhaps you want to move to a more affordable area or to be closer to your children. Or you're thinking about eventually choosing a retirement community that you can move into for life and that will provide more than just a place to live.

Write down some of the qualities you think you'll want as you start exploring the possibilities. You and your spouse could each make a list and then compare them to see how close you are to agreeing on what you want.

The majority of retirees who have moved during the last few decades have chosen Florida, California and Arizona. But recently Texas, North Carolina, Washington and Virginia have increased in popularity. A place in one of these popular retirement havens might suit your needs. Or maybe you'll discover a haven of your own, here or in another country altogether.

Resources That Can Help

Whether you're unsure if there actually *is* a place that fits your somewhat vague notion of what you want or you've got some specific places in mind that you'd like to compare,

these resources will tell you what you need to know.
- *Retirement Places Rated* ($19.95; Macmillan Travel), by David Savageau, provides data on cost of living, housing, climate and crime for 183 popular places for retirement. The book ranks them by each category of information so you can see how your choices compare to other places around the country. Savageau also considers all the factors to give an overall ranking to the communities.
- *Places Rated Almanac* software ($39.95; PHH Technology Services, 800-210-8852) gives computer users the ability to study the same statistics on even more places. Although the software hasn't been updated since 1993 (a new version will be released in 1997), it gives you a general idea of how the cost of living and other factors compare among 343 metropolitan areas in the U.S. and Canada.

    The software lets you sort the cities according to size, region of the country and other criteria. For example, if you're looking for a city on the Pacific Coast with a population between 100,000 and 200,000, Bellingham, Wash., is ranked best overall. But if you make medical services the most important factor, Medford-Ashland, Ore., comes out on top. The software is easy to use and also provides phone numbers for getting more information about each city.
- *Where to Retire* ($14.95; Gateway Books, 2023 Clemens Road, Oakland, CA 94602; 800-669-0773), by John Howells, goes beyond statistics to give the author's subjective opinion about many popular retirement locales. Based on his travels and interviews, Howells describes the quality of life in towns and cities from Florida to Hawaii, focusing primarily on the southern half of the country. The book also includes statistics on weather, costs and crime.
- *Choose the Southwest* and *Choose the Northwest* ($12.95 each; Gateway Books, see above), also by John Howells, focus on two popular regions for retirees. *Choose the Southwest* covers Arizona, Colorado, Nevada, New Mexico, Western Texas and Utah; *Choose the Northwest* includes Washington, Oregon and British Columbia. Both contain information on cost of living, housing, climate, health care and more for many of the large communities in these regions.

- *Where to Retire* magazine ($11.95 for four quarterly issues; Vacation Publications, 1502 Augusta Drive, Suite 415, Houston, TX 77057; 713–974–6903) is another good resource. Issues include profiles of cities and articles discussing tax or health issues that may factor into your decision.
- Vacation Publications also publishes *America's Most Affordable Retirement Towns* ($3.95), which provides statistics and commentary on 25 towns around the country that offer a combination of low living costs and good quality of life, and *America's Best Places to Retire* ($14.95 plus $2.25 shipping and handling), which is a collection of 149 city profiles reprinted from its magazine. Another useful offering: *Tax Heaven or Hell* ($11.95), by Eve Evans and Alan Fox. It's a thorough book on state taxes that includes a ranking of 149 metropolitan areas and popular retirement towns by the tax burden they place on retirees.
- *State Tax Policy & Senior Citizens* ($25; National Conference of State Legislatures, 1560 Broadway, Suite 700, Denver, CO 80202; 303–830–2054) is another good source for state tax information. It provides an in-depth look at state income, property, sales and estate taxes, and what relief is available for seniors in each state.

If your search for the perfect retirement locale will extend beyond the borders of the U.S., these tours and resources can help.
- Lifestyle Explorations (101 Federal Street, Suite 1900, Boston, MA 02110; 508–371–4814) offers nine- to 13-day tours of seven countries it considers good choices for retirees in terms of cost of living and lifestyle. The countries are Argentina, Canada's Maritime provinces, Costa Rica, Honduras, Ireland, Portugal and Uruguay. In addition to sightseeing, you'll tour residential areas with a local realtor, visit some Americans living there and learn about day-to-day life in these countries.
- *Retire in Mexico Updates & Business News* (40 Fourth Street, Suite 204, Petaluma, CA 94952; 800–570–6111) offers four living and investment tours per year to Lake Chapala and

other popular communities in Mexico. These escorted educational tours offer personal introductions to people within the community, networking opportunities, dinners in private homes, and presentations by local authorities on immigration issues, health care, banking and real estate.
- *The World's Top Retirement Havens* ($19.97 plus $2 shipping; Agora Publishing, 105 West Monument Street, Baltimore, MD 21201; 800–981–3818) examines what it's like to retire in popular places such as Bermuda, France and Mexico, and some you might not expect, like Poland and Switzerland. The book is a mix of information about climate and geography, the native populations, living costs and laws pertaining to visiting, moving or becoming a citizen.
- Agora Publishing also puts out a monthly newsletter, *International Living* ($34 for one year), for people who are interested in relocating, traveling extensively or investing in other countries. The newsletter also announces the Discovery Tours of countries such as Honduras, Mexico, Nicaragua, Belize and Ireland. Originally available only to newsletter subscribers, these tours are now available to everyone (call 800–926–6575).
- *Choose Mexico* ($11.95; Gateway Books, 2023 Clemens Road, Oakland, CA 94602; 800–669–0773) and *Choose Costa Rica* ($13.95; Gateway Books), by John Howells, offer a variety of useful information about relocating to those countries.
- *Retiring Outside the United States* ($3.95; Vacation Publications, see *Where to Retire* magazine on the preceding page) provides general advice on issues such as language differences, transportation, owning property and paying taxes. It also discusses the specifics of Mexico, Costa Rica, Algarve in Portugal, Canada's Maritime provinces, Uruguay, Ireland and Venezuela.

Choosing Your New Home

Once you've narrowed your search down to a few possibilities there are several things you should do to find out more about those places so that you can make your choice. You really can't do too much research in preparation for making this kind of move; realizing you've made a bad decision is likely to be very costly, both financially and emotionally.

Get More Information

In addition to using resources such as those mentioned above, write or call the state or local chamber of commerce and tourism offices for more information. Also, consider subscribing to—or at least getting several editions of—the local paper(s) so you can see what issues are of concern to the people who live there.

Make Several Visits

Spend at least a week in these places during several different times of the year. Some places that attract a lot of tourism during certain times of the year may be very different during the off season, both in terms of weather and the social and entertainment scene. When you're visiting, focus on the things that will be important to you as a resident, such as the quality and variety of housing and the accessibility of hospitals and medical centers. Also, pay attention to transportation issues. How far away are the nearest major highway, airport and train station?

Check whether the place offers the type of entertainment and leisure activities you enjoy. A rural area where outdoor recreation, county fairs and farmers' markets are the main attractions might be fun, but if you're used to ready access to quality museums and theater, you may miss those after a while.

Look at Demographics

Ask the local chambers of commerce for demographic information about the areas, such as the average level of income and educational achievement. That will give you a general sense of the local residents. If most of the people in the community make significantly more or less than you do, for example, you may find that puts a strain on socializing with them.

Crunch the Numbers

If finding a place where you'll have a significantly lower cost of living is the main reason you want to relocate, do a careful comparison of the taxes, housing costs and other living expenses in the areas you're considering.

If you want professional help with this, Right Choice (151 Woodland Meade, Suite 4, South Hamilton, MA 01982; 800–872–2294), a relocation consulting firm, will do a personalized analysis of the changes you can expect in your budget due to a move. The cost is $190 for a comparison with one city or town and half the price for a second city. You fill out a 22-page questionnaire on your personal finances, for which you'll need the up-to-date figures on how much you spend on food, travel utilities, etc., that you compiled on page 38. Many of the questions are geared toward salary and job-related expenses; those can be left blank if you won't be working any more after you move. Right Choice also offers software called *ReloSmart* ($79.99; Windows, DOS or Macintosh) that lets you do the same type of analysis on your own using data on 600 cities. But again, it's designed for people who will be earning income from a job after they move, and the results you get will not reflect changes in your tax bill because of social security or pension income or tax breaks states may give for those types of income.

No matter how much research you do, there are things you won't discover about the place until you're actually living there. When you've made your final choice, rent a home in the area for six months to a year before you buy property there. You'll give yourself time to uncover problems or annoyances that you didn't foresee during your shorter visits.

Considering a Retirement Community

As part of your long-range retirement planning, you may be considering the idea of moving into a retirement community at some point. As people age, they are often attracted to this type of housing for a number of reasons: the security and services these communities provide; the opportunity to live among people of the same age who share their interests and outlook; the easy access to medical care; and the health-care and long-term care coverage that's sometimes provided. Many people feel that they're relieving their adult children of the burden of having to care for them or provide financial support later in life if they can buy into a community that will provide all the care they're likely to need. Most retirement housing fits into one of these three general categories.

Independent Living

These communities offer houses, apartments, condominiums, cooperatives, mobile homes or some combination to retirees (usually they are restricted to people over 45 or 55) who can take care of themselves. Most offer recreational facilities and planned activities. The availability of other services, such as outdoor maintenance and on-location shopping and banking, varies from place to place.

Assisted Living

These facilities provide a combination of housing, support services and some health care for people who need help with activities of daily living—including dressing, cooking and bathing—but don't need the round-the-clock care provided by a nursing home.

Continuing Care/Life Care

These communities offer a mix of living arrangements and services designed to provide what you may need as you age. They usually include independent-living apartments or cottages, assisted living housing, a medical center and skilled-nursing home facilities all at one location. At some facilities, you can sign a contract that guarantees residence and care for life; others provide care on a pay-as-you-go basis.

Continuing-care Retirement Communities (CCRCs) are fast becoming the most popular and prevalent type of retirement housing because of the full range of options that's usually available. There are more than 1,000 non-profit and for-profit CCRCs around the country, but the most desirable and established communities have waiting lists of one or two years, or more, for their larger independent-living units. So if you think this is something you may want in the future, start shopping for a community several years before you plan to move in. You'll also want to have plenty of time to make your decision because the requirements, choices, contracts and restrictions associated with these communities are extremely complex.

The entry requirements for CCRCs vary, but in most cases you must be relatively healthy, and you must pay either a non-refundable or partially refundable entry fee, plus a monthly charge for your housing, meal plan and any health care provided. Monthly charges may be relatively low if entry fees are high enough to cover anticipated future costs, but you'll likely pay much more per month in communities with fairly low initial fees. On average, one-time entrance fees range from about $60,000 to $120,000 and monthly charges from $1,000 to $1,600 per person. One-time fees and monthly charges may be less on a per-person basis for double-occupancy housing.

Incoming residents also must have enough resources to cover anticipated expenses so CCRCs look into the health and financial status of each applicant and may require residents to submit annual financial statements or to sign agreements to not give away needed assets in the future.

CCRCs offer residents access to a broad array of health care and many provide a variety of plans to suit different types of needs. For example, your health may preclude you from the community's most comprehensive health-care plan, but your spouse may be able to sign up for it while you get coverage under a fee-for-service plan. The contract you sign when you move into the community governs exactly what care you're entitled to and how much you will have to pay. Have a lawyer review the contract before you sign to help you understand your health-care coverage.

These are the three most common continuing-care plans.
- **Life care (extensive).** A life-care agreement is the most comprehensive and the most expensive plan. It guarantees you access—on a pre-paid basis—to certain assisted-living support and nursing care as long as you live in the community. Some life-care plans also may cover routine care,

such as visits to the community's nurse or clinic. Extensive contracts offer you the most security. About 40% of nonprofit communities offer them.
- *Fee-for-service.* With this plan, you are promised access to services but pay for a CCRC's assisted-living and nursing care as you use them. New communities are more likely to offer fee-for-service agreements, and roughly 40% of CCRCs have them.
- *Modified.* This type of plan usually combines some prepaid health care with a fee-for-service arrangement. About a third of nonprofit CCRCs offer modified contracts. What a modified plan pays for varies tremendously from one CCRC to another. If the community has assisted-living quarters and a nursing-care center on the premises, the contract should set out in detail the cost and conditions for obtaining access to them.

Many CCRCs also incorporate long-term-care insurance into their plans (see page 119 for more on this insurance) either with a group policy that residents must qualify for in order to move in or by offering residents the opportunity to buy individual policies at group rates. The following resources can provide more information, and help with locating retirement communities in the areas where you want to live.
- *The Consumers' Directory of Continuing Care Retirement Communities* ($24.95 plus $3.50 for shipping; American Association of Homes and Services for the Aging, or AAHSA, Publications, Dept. 5119, Washington, DC 20061-5119; 800–508–9442 or 301–490–0677) contains information on hundreds of CCRCs around the country, explains how CCRCs work and provides suggestions on what to look for and what to ask before making your choice. Regional editions of the directory may be available in 1997.

AAHSA also publishes a free *Accredited Facilities List* brochure each year of the CCRCs that have been accredited by AAHSA's Continuing Care Accreditation Commission, which is made up of CCRC providers and consumer representatives.

- *The Directory of Retirement Facilities*, published annually by Health Care Information Analysts, Inc. (800–568–3282), lists more than 22,000 facilities nationwide, including retirement communities and nursing homes. The entries list basic contact information, types of living arrangements offered, entry and monthly fees, the number of units and residents, whether the facility is for-profit or not-for-profit and more. The directory is some 1,400 pages and costs $249 (plus $7.95 shipping and handling). However, it's available in many libraries.
- Area Agencies on Aging (AAAs) can also help you find out what's available in your city or state. They can often provide lists of local retirement communities and assisted-living facilities, or refer you to other resources. To locate the AAA for your community, check the blue government pages in your phone book or look in the yellow pages under "Aging" or "Senior Citizens." Or call Eldercare Locator (800–677–1116), a public service funded by the U.S. Administration on Aging, which will refer you to any local agencies or organizations that will help you locate the retirement housing you're seeking.
- *The 50 Best Retirement Communities in America* ($14.95; St. Martin's Press, 800–288–2131), by Alice and Fred Lee, discusses the pluses and minuses of the authors' favorite communities based on their travels and interviews with residents and staff. It includes a section on military, religious and college-affiliated communities.

Chapter 13

Enjoying Your Leisure

If you plan for it well, retirement will be a time when you can finally do the things you've always wanted to do, but never had time for before. Whether it be taking on volunteer work for a cause in which you strongly believe, using your creative talents to learn a new hobby, or returning to the classroom for a degree or just the joy of learning (page 92), retirement can be an opportunity to find fulfillment in totally new ways. You may already have something in mind and know how to go about getting started. But if you don't, this chapter will give you an idea of many meaningful and creative ways you can make the most of your retirement years.

Volunteering Your Time and Skills

Retirees represent the country's most abundant source of volunteers. Almost half of all people age 60 and older spend part of their free time helping others, according to a study by Marriott Senior Living Services, the division of Marriott that operates its retirement communities. The opportunities are plentiful, from becoming a volunteer driver for Meals-on-Wheels to leading nature tours at a national park to helping children learn. Some volunteer work requires special skills and experience, but many more programs call for nothing but energy, caring and enthusiasm. Here is a sampling of programs that might appeal to your interests.

Use a Volunteer Clearinghouse

These programs can match your skills and interests to groups or individuals that need your help. Schools, religious institutions, hospitals and social service agencies are also good places to start looking for volunteer opportunities in your area.

- ***AARP Volunteer Talent Bank*** (601 E Street, N.W., Washington, DC 20049) is a database that can match volunteers with the American Association of Retired Persons' own service programs, such as its 55 Alive/Mature Driving course for people over age 50, or with a number of national organizations, including the American Red Cross and Recording for the Blind.
- ***Retired and Senior Volunteer Program (RSVP)*** connects more than 455,000 people age 55 and older with volunteer opportunities nationwide. The program, which is administered by the Corporation for National and Community Service, is coordinated on the local level by public agencies or non-profit groups—often the United Way. It recruits volunteers in that community and refers them to local organizations that need volunteers. RSVP volunteers do all kinds of work, from teaching English as a second language to serving as a docent in a museum. Check your local phone directory for the RSVP program nearest you. If there's no local listing, see if there's a program located in your state's capital city or visit RSVP's website at www.cns.gov.
- ***The National Park Service*** (Division of Interpretation, P.O. Box 37127, Washington, DC 20013; 202–523–5270) uses volunteers, mostly retirees, for all kinds of tasks—working at an information desk, maintaining trails, guiding tours, etc. You can volunteer as many or as few hours as you like, on a seasonal basis or year-round. For an information brochure, write to the National Park Service at the address above.

Provide Business Help

If you spend 30 years or more developing and honing skills in a particular field, chances are someone could benefit from your expertise—from a non-profit organization or a struggling young entrepreneur to a newly privatized factory in Russia. If you're interested in sharing your knowledge in the U.S. or abroad, these programs can arrange it.

- ***National Executive Service Corps*** (257 Park Ave. South, New York, NY 10010; 212–529–6660) is a management consulting organization with affiliates in 39 cities across the country that matches retired business managers and executives with social service agencies, schools, cultural and performing arts organizations, health-care agencies, environmental groups and other nonprofits. Volunteers are needed in many areas, including strategic and business planning, management information systems and fundraising strategies. A typical volunteer consultant might work two days a week on a project lasting four to six months. By helping an organization become better managed, volunteers ensure that more of its scarce resources go toward programs supporting the group's mission.

- ***Service Corps of Retired Executives*** (SCORE; 800–634–0245) has 12,300 volunteers in local Small Business Administration offices all over the country (see page 91). SCORE counselors advise small business owners about such things as writing a business plan, marketing a new product and exporting. They also conduct business workshops for would-be business owners. Women and minority counselors and volunteers with computer skills are especially needed.

- ***Emeritus Foundation*** (1614 20th Street, N.W., Washington, DC 20009; 202–232–0863) sends retired teachers, managers, lawyers, scientists, mathematicians and engineers to work in local schools and other community agencies in the Washington, D.C., area. There is no age limit.

Make a Difference in a Child's Life

Your days of changing diapers, helping with homework and going to PTA meetings may be over, but you can still play a significant role in the lives of young people.

- ***Help One Student to Succeed*** (8000 Northeast Parkway Dr., #201, Vancouver, WA 98662; 800–833–4678) is a

mentoring program in 800 schools nationwide that works to improve reading, writing and study skills of students in elementary and secondary schools.
- ***Foster Grandparent Program*** (800–424–8867) recruits members to help infants abandoned at birth, addicted to drugs and those who are HIV-positive. They assist children and adolescents with learning disabilities, those who have been abused, neglected, or are in the juvenile justice system. Members also help teen parents and their children.
- ***Family Friends*** (409 Third Street, S.W., Second Floor, Washington, DC 20024; 202–479–6675) is a national senior volunteer program that brings older volunteers—generally 55 and older—into the homes of children who are medically fragile or who need special services. A Family Friend becomes a surrogate grandparent to the child, siblings and parents who welcome them. The program is sponsored by The National Council on The Aging.
- ***Help local schools*** by encouraging local businesses to donate needed school supplies such as science lab, art or sports equipment. For additional ideas, contact the National Association of Partners in Education (901 N. Pitt Street, #320, Alexandria, VA 22314; 703–836–4880).
- *Golden Opportunities: A Volunteer Guide For Americans Over 50* ($14.95 plus $4.75 for shipping; Peterson's Customer Service, P.O. Box 2123, Princeton, NJ 08543; 800–338–3282) lists hundreds of volunteer opportunities, from helping needy children to feeding the hungry. It describes a wide array of volunteer organizations, complete with addresses and phone numbers. It also profiles some older volunteers who have made a change for the better in the lives of others and in their own lives.

Starting a New Hobby

It's probably been a long time since you had enough spare time to work on a hobby. There were probably things you liked to do as a kid or a young adult—maybe you built model railroads, played the piano, tracked the stars and planets with a telescope or developed your own photographs.

But as the responsibilities of work and raising a family took up more of your time and energy, these interests were probably neglected.

As you plan for retirement, think of it as your golden opportunity to renew old interests or develop new hobbies and skills that use your creative energy. If you're not sure what kind of thing you want to try, you'll find there's no shortage of hobby stores and how-to books waiting to inspire you.

Explore possibilities by visiting a local library or bookstore, or attending adult-education workshops at community colleges, high schools or hobby organizations. Hobby- and craft-supply stores can also provide inspiration, and some post notices about classes, meetings or outings for hobby enthusiasts. As you search for the right hobby, keep your personality, aptitude and income in mind. But if a hobby requires costly equipment and materials, it may be possible to get access to equipment on a shared basis through community centers, schools and clubs. Or you can often purchase second-hand equipment at a fraction of the retail cost.

There's no reason to limit yourself to just one hobby if you come across several things that interest you. In fact, you may find you enjoy having several hobbies so that you can move from one to the other as your mood or interests change. If you develop a hobby that you do extremely well, you may find that people you know are willing to pay for your work. Making money from your hobby could be an added bonus down the road, but going into it with the intention of earning money could take away from your enjoyment of the hobby itself.

Part 5

Protecting Your Assets

Even the most well-crafted retirement plan could be jeopardized by large expenses for which you are not prepared. A serious accident or illness in retirement could be a huge drain on your nest egg if you don't have adequate health insurance. A stroke, Alzheimer's disease or another debilitating health problem could leave you or your spouse needing expensive home care or care in a nursing home for many years. The average annual cost of nursing home care in the United States is currently $39,000. And if you die prematurely, without planning for how your assets should be distributed to your survivors, estate taxes and legal fees could leave your spouse without enough, or drastically reduce the amount you intend to leave behind for your children and grandchildren.

While you can't protect yourself from the emotional impact such events might have on you or your family, you can cushion the financial blow to your retirement savings.

The proper mix of planning, insurance, legal tools and professional help can make a big difference in how well you'll be able to cope with unforeseeable expenses and needs. It's wise, not pessimistic, to plan for the worst—you and your family will be glad that you did.

Chapter 14

A Health Care Safety Net

Continuing increases in medical costs and longer life spans have made solid and affordable health insurance coverage vital for everyone. And once you retire, adequate health insurance will be even more important because you're likely to see your medical expenses become a larger part of your budget as you age (see page 39). For that reason, make sure that you'll have appropriate coverage throughout your retirement years—before you qualify for medicare at age 65, if you retire early, and after 65, when you'll need additional coverage to pick up where medicare leaves off.

Your Employer's Plan

The rising cost of health insurance has forced some employers to scale back or drop the coverage they provide to employees—particularly to their retired employees. A recent study by the Pension Benefits and Welfare Administration, part of the U.S. Department of Labor, found that only 34% of retirees age 55 and older had coverage under the health plan of their former employer and that only 30% indicated that the coverage could be continued for life.

The good news is that the number of employers cutting back or dumping health benefits for retired workers has now leveled off. But more and more, companies that do provide retiree health benefits are switching to less-expensive managed-care plans and raising the share that retirees must pay for their coverage.

If you're planning to retire before medicare kicks in at age 65, you need to be sure you can secure health coverage until it does. If you and your spouse are both working and will have health benefits in retirement, compare what each of your companies offers to determine which is the better deal. Many companies will cover retirees' spouses at an additional cost, but usually that option is available only if the spouse is enrolled in the plan before the employee retires. And sometimes your spouse must be in your plan for a certain number of years before you retire in order to qualify.

If you're retiring early because your employer is encouraging you to retire, push for lifetime health insurance for you and your spouse to be included in the buyout offer. (See page 52 for more on early retirement packages.)

Once you become eligible for medicare, many employers switch your coverage to medicare supplemental insurance—also known as "medigap" coverage—or at least share part of the cost of buying a policy. This type of insurance covers medicare deductibles and co-payments and picks up some of the costs that medicare won't. (More on medigap insurance on page 116.)

If you retire before age 65 and neither you nor your spouse has employer-provided coverage, you have a few other options, but none of them will be cheap. It's important to shop around to make sure you get adequate coverage at the best possible price. Starting in mid 1997, health-reform legislation should make it easier for people in that situation to buy health insurance on the individual market. Under the new legislation, anyone who's been covered by an employer's plan or COBRA (see below) for at least 18 months prior to shopping for a policy is guaranteed coverage on the individual market without being subject to limitations for preexisting conditions. At least two different policies must be available to these people in every state, but affordability will vary from state to state. In some states, the new rules won't take effect until 1998.

Another option for early retirees without coverage is to take advantage of the Consolidated Omnibus Budget Reconciliation Act of 1985—better known as COBRA. This law says that if your employer provides coverage and has at least 20 employees, you're eligible to stay under that group coverage for up to 18 months after you leave the job. You'll have to pay the full cost of the insurance plus a fee, but it'll likely be cheaper than buying an individual policy.

Managed care is an even more affordable way to cover yourself and your spouse, if you're willing to give up a lot of flexibility. Many health maintenance organizations (HMOs) have open enrollment periods when they'll accept anyone.

In addition, some people who are members of professional or religious groups may be able to get group coverage through the association. For example, B'nai B'rith offers group coverage to members.

For more help with finding affordable health insurance, contact your state insurance commissioner's office. It should be able to tell you what's available locally and may even provide a list of insurers. Look for that listing in your phone book or access state insurance commissioner phone numbers and addresses online at www.naic.org, the National Association of Insurance Commissioners' website.

Understanding Medicare

Once you turn 65, the federal health insurance program known as medicare starts picking up part of your medical expenses. Medicare, which is administered by the Health Care Financing Administration (HCFA), is split into two parts: Part A, which is hospital insurance, and Part B, which is supplemental medical insurance. Medicare beneficiaries must pay various deductibles and co-payments before coverage kicks in. For example, medicare pays all the costs for up to 60 days in the hospital after a $760 (in 1997) deductible. For hospital days 61 to 90 in 1997, all costs are covered after a $190 per day co-payment. Days 91 to 150 are covered after a $380 per day co-payment (in 1997), and for days 151+, medicare pays nothing. You also pay a premium for Part B, which was $43.80 per month in 1997.

In addition, there are a variety of expenses that medicare doesn't cover at all. For example, medicare pays nothing for prescription drugs, routine physical exams, dental care, hearing exams and hearing aids, or vision exams and eyeglasses, except after cataract surgery. To find out more about what medicare does and doesn't pay, get a free copy of *Your Medicare Handbook* at your local social security office. It's also available on the Internet at HCFA's website, www.hcfa.gov. For additional information, call HCFA's toll-free information line (800–638–6833). You can also get help from your state's medicare carriers, which are listed in the back of the *Handbook*.

Although about 90% of medicare beneficiaries still receive care from this traditional medicare fee-for-service program, medicare managed care options are becoming increasingly available as a replacement for medicare and medigap coverage. Medicare HMOs are required to provide the same services that are available under regular medicare, except for hospice coverage. But many HMOs also offer additional coverage for services, including eye exams, hearing aids and partial prescription drug coverage. With HMOs, you must use a primary care physician from the plan's network, but there is none of the paperwork that is involved with regular medicare and only nominal co-payments are required. There are also more flexible managed care options available for medicare beneficiaries, including point-of-service HMOs, which allow you to use doctors outside of the network at additional cost, and a program called Medicare Select, an option similar to a preferred provider organization (PPO) that can replace medigap coverage.

For more information on medicare managed care, consult *Your Medicare Handbook* or get a copy of *Medicare HMOs: Some Tips for Consumers* ($2; United Seniors Health Cooperative, 1331 H Street, N.W., Suite 500, Washington, DC 20005-4706; 202–393–6222).

Choosing Medigap Coverage

Because the traditional medicare program requires you to pay a lot out-of-pocket and doesn't cover many services, you should buy medicare supplement insurance to fill in the gaps. Medigap insurance is privately sold, and federal rules that took effect in 1992 have made comparing policies a lot easier. For six months after you sign up for medicare Part B, you can choose any medigap policy you want and, regardless of your health, the company must cover you. But after that six-month window has closed, companies aren't obligated to accept you. If, after you've already purchased medigap coverage, you want to switch to a different policy, there's no waiting period for preexisting conditions.

Under the 1992 rules, each medigap policy must conform to one of ten defined packages of benefits, which are labeled A through J. The ten plans give you a variety of choices, but you can probably narrow your search to four: A, D, G and H.

- **Policy A** is the least expensive and should be the most competitively priced of the ten packages because all companies must offer it. It pays for hospital charges that are not covered by medicare after a 60-day stay, up to 150 days. It also covers the full cost of up to 365 additional hospital days during your lifetime, the co-payment for medicare's allowed amount for physician charges, and the first three pints of blood yearly (medicare coverage takes over after that). Policy A is a good choice if your aim is to cover only catastrophic costs.
- **Policy D** covers everything included with A and pays your hospital deductible, adds some coverage for custodial care at home following an illness or injury and covers the co-payment for skilled nursing-home care. It also pays for foreign travel emergency care.
- **Policy G** provides the same coverage as policy D, plus it pays the fees for nonparticipating physicians—doctors who charge more than the amount approved by medicare.
- **Policy H** is the least-expensive package that includes some basic prescription-drug coverage. The other coverage it provides is the same as policy D except it does not include the coverage for custodial care at home.

Low-income retirees might want to consider policy B, which costs more than policy A but covers the hospital deductible—a valuable benefit for someone on a tight budget.

For more information about choosing a medigap policy, get a copy of *Medicare, Medigap and Managed Care: 1997 Consumer Update* ($3.50; United Seniors Health Cooperative, see address on page 116). Another helpful publication is *Guide to Health Insurance for People with Medicare*, published by the Health Care Financing Administration. Free copies should be available from your state's insurance department (listed in the government pages of your phone book). Also, the Medicare Rights Center (1460 Broadway, 8th Floor, Box A, New York, NY 10036) offers a publication called *Medicare HMOs 1996* ($3) in addition to a number of other low-cost publications on medicare. Write to request a complete list.

Free health insurance counseling programs, funded by the federal government, are available on the state level. You can get advice over the phone or in person, as well as written materials to help with claims, appeals and more. Contact information for each state's counseling program is listed in the back of *Your Medicare Handbook*. Or call Eldercare Locator (800–677–1116) and ask about your state's program.

Chapter 15

Do You Need Long-Term-Care Insurance?

If some time in the future you or your spouse need long-term care at home or in an assisted-living facility or nursing home, the cost of this care is likely to put a strain on your finances that may leave the other spouse with very little for day-to-day living. Medicare and your medigap policy won't cover enough of this care to protect you financially, and medicaid—the federal-state program that covers more of the nursing home costs for Americans than any other type of coverage—will become more and more difficult to qualify for as requirements are tightened to keep the program afloat financially.

These concerns are driving many retirees into the long-term-care insurance market to buy some protection for themselves, their family and their assets. Although long-term-care insurance has improved a great deal during the years it has been on the market, consumers still need to consider all their options first and be very careful about making this purchase.

What Medicare Covers

Before you start looking at long-term-care insurance, you should understand what medicare covers in this area. Medicare Part A will help pay for medically necessary care in a skilled nursing home or in your home, but only if you've been hospitalized for at least three days prior to entering the home and are being admitted for the same condition for which you were hospitalized. Also, a doctor must certify that you need medical care on a daily basis and the nursing home must be a medicare-approved facility. If your needs are strictly custodial—help with everyday tasks such as eating, walking and bathing—medicare won't pay.

But even if you qualify for skilled nursing coverage, medicare pays in full for only the first 20 days of covered services. For days 21 through 100, you must pay a co-payment ($95 per day in 1997) and then medicare will pick up the rest. After 100 days, you are responsible for the whole bill. Because of the limited nature of this coverage, medicare pays only about 2% of all nursing home costs.

What will medigap insurance cover? Not a whole lot more. Policies C through J (as mentioned on page 117) pay your skilled nursing co-payment for days 21 through 100, but the policies offer no additional long-term-care coverage, other than the limited at-home custodial care following an illness, surgery or injury that's included in policies D, G, I and J.

Medicaid, the "payer of last resort" for long-term care, picks up a lot of the bill for many people who need long-term nursing home care. However, you have to spend your assets down to almost nothing in order to qualify and, as we mentioned before, the program is likely to become even more restrictive as efforts are made to save the program by shifting more of the responsibility for it to the states.

Who Needs Insurance?

The cost of long-term care can be devastating, but the risk of ending up in a nursing home is often exaggerated. A 65-year-old's chances of being in a home at some point range from about 20% to 50%, depending on the study you're consulting. And that sounds worse than it is because studies often include short-term nursing-home stays that occur after hospitalization—the kind that are likely to be covered by medicare.

The point to keep in mind is that you really shouldn't buy long-term-care (LTC) insurance if it's going to put a major strain on your retirement budget. A good rule of thumb is that no more than 10% of your annual income should go to paying LTC insurance premiums. The United Seniors Health Cooperative, a nonprofit consumer organization that provides information and guidance on health issues for retirees (see page 116), suggests buying the insurance only if you meet the following guidelines:

- You have more than $75,000 in assets per person in your household (not including your residence).
- Your annual income is $30,000 or more per person.
- You can afford the premiums without making lifestyle changes.
- You could still afford the premiums if they increase by 20% to 30% in the future.

By the same token, don't assume that you should buy LTC insurance just because you can afford it. If your net worth is $1 million or more, you may do better by self-insuring—setting aside money to pay for whatever care you may need in the future.

Another thing to keep in mind: Couples need LTC insurance more than single people do. That's because if one spouse ends up in a nursing home, it's likely to deplete the couple's assets and leave almost nothing for the other. But if you're single or have a high net worth, you still might want the insurance if it's important to you that some of your assets be preserved for your heirs or for charity.

The best time to purchase LTC insurance is in your 60s. You may be encouraged to buy in your 50s because the premiums will be lower, but keep in mind that you'll be paying the premiums for a longer period of time. If you wait until you're over 70, it may be more difficult to get the policy you want, and the premiums could be significantly higher.

Choosing a Policy

More than 125 companies are currently selling long-term-care insurance, but many are not worthy of your consideration. To make sure you choose a company that offers a wide variety of policies at reasonable prices, and that the policy you buy will be there when you need it, heed the following suggestions:

Go with a Sound Company

Look for a company that has been in business a long time and has top ratings from at least two rating agencies, such as A.M. Best, Standard & Poor's and Moody's. (See page 32 for more on checking these ratings.)

Look for Broad Coverage

New policies from the better companies include coverage for home care, assisted living, adult day care, Alzheimer's disease care units and other alternatives to nursing homes. If these services are readily available in your community, this coverage could make sense for you.

Read the Policy

Don't rely on an agent's description or an "outline of coverage" document. Fine points in the language of the policy can make a big difference. For example, a policy may say it covers Alzheimer's disease, but contain provisions that require "medical necessity," "cognitive impairment" and the "inability to perform activities of daily living" in order to receive benefits. Alzheimer's patients can often physically perform these activities—such as bathing or dressing—but don't know where or when to do them. They may also have no "medical" problems.

When you get into reading and comparing the details of the policies you're considering, these points will help you sort out the good and the bad:

What to Look for

Inflation protection is an important feature that usually comes in several forms. Most increase your daily benefit over time to keep up with the rising cost of care. The best—but most expensive—type is one that raises your benefit each year at a compounded rate of 5% for the life of the policy. You can also choose to have the benefit raised for a stated number of years or until you reach a certain age. Inflation protection is most important for people who are in good health, have a family history of longevity and aren't likely to need long-term care for at least ten years.

Home care coverage pays a flat dollar amount per day to cover help with personal care (bathing, dressing, etc.) and skilled care from nurses and therapists in your home. But if the benefit usually pays for only a few hours of care per day, it's not worth the extra expense unless you'll definitely have a spouse, relative or friend who will be capable of caring for you the rest of the time.

What to Avoid

Medical-necessity provisions are bad news. Don't buy policies that tie the payment of your benefits to medical or health problems. You may need care due to mental or physical disabilities that are caused by old age, not a specific illness or injury. Also, the policy should mention both cognitive and physical disabilities, but you shouldn't need both to receive your benefits.

A nonforfeiture benefit lets you retain some value in your policy (or gives you a refund of part of your premiums) if you let the policy lapse. Adding this feature can increase your premiums by as much as 50% to 100%. You're better off buying affordable coverage that you'll be able to maintain until you need care.

Restoration of benefits is another feature you can do without. Say you buy a policy that will pay benefits for three years. If you are in a nursing home for a year and then don't need care again for six months, this feature ensures that your full three-year benefit period will be restored. Because people who spend as long as a year in a nursing home tend to remain there the rest of their lives, you're unlikely to benefit from this feature.

Premiums that are a lot cheaper than similar offerings you've seen can be a red flag. Either the company may be planning to raise the premiums substantially, or it's not pricing the policy accurately and won't have the funds to pay your benefits when you need them.

Get Counseling

You may find yourself overwhelmed by the task of deciphering and comparing LTC policies. Instead of just getting help from an agent, who has a financial interest in your decision, ask your area agency on aging or state insurance department about LTC insurance counseling in your area. Eldercare Locator (800–677–1116) can put you in touch with your state's health insurance counseling program (all states are required to have one).

For more information on long-term-care insurance, consult the following resources:

- *Private Long Term Care Insurance: To Buy or Not to Buy?* ($2; United Seniors Health Cooperative, see address on page 116) is a four-page report on the key issues involved in making the decision. Also from United Seniors Health Cooperative: *Long Term Care Insurance: A Professional's Guide to Selecting Policies* ($41), a 145-page book covering all the options for funding long-term care and the fine points of selecting the right policy, is useful for knowledgeable consumers as well as professionals. And *Long-term Care Planning: A Dollar and Sense Guide* ($13), an 80-page booklet covering private long-term-care insurance, self insuring, reverse mortgages and creative living arrangements.
- The American Association of Retired Persons (AARP Fulfillment, 601 E Street NW, Washington, DC 20049) publishes *Before You Buy: A Guide to Long-Term Care Insurance* and other free booklets on nursing homes, home care and other health issues.

Chapter 16

A Plan for Your Estate

The final touch on a solid retirement plan is to make arrangements for how your assets should be distributed to your heirs after you're gone. A thorough estate plan not only means a lot less trouble and uncertainty for your survivors; it can also mean saving on estate taxes and legal fees that can take a significant bite out of your estate.

According to a recent Merrill Lynch survey of more than 800 people age 45 and older, 40% of respondents thought that estate planning was necessary only in a complex family or financial situation, and 27% thought that using professionals to develop an estate plan is only for the very rich. In this chapter, we'll try to dispel these and other misconceptions about estate planning and help you decide what tools you need to meet the goals you have for your estate.

Assessing Your Need for Life Insurance

For most Americans, buying life insurance was their first step toward providing for their survivors in the event of their death. But once you retire, you may find that you don't need life insurance anymore and that the money you're spending on premiums could be better spent elsewhere. Or you may find that life insurance can play a new and different role in your estate plan.

One of the main reasons people buy life insurance is to replace their income so that their dependent survivors will have enough to live on after they're gone. The people who need the most insurance are those with young children. Once your children are grown, you may need only enough insurance to support your spouse. But many families today find themselves supporting aging parents as well.

How much insurance you need depends on how much income your dependents will have after you're gone. Review your policies to determine if you have enough insurance to cover any reduction in your dependents' income that would result from your death. If you have saved and invested well, you may not need that much life insurance because your assets will provide the protection they'll need.

Why You Might Still Need It

If you don't need the life insurance you have for income replacement, you may want to keep or add to your insurance for one of the following reasons:

- **Estate planning.** If your biggest assets are your home, a small business, real estate or other illiquid investments, life insurance can provide the cash your heirs will need to cover any estate taxes. In addition, if qualified retirement accounts—such as IRAs, 401(k)s and Keoghs—are a big part of your estate, you'll want life insurance to cover the estate taxes on those so that they won't have to be cashed out to pay it. For married couples, estate taxes aren't due until the second spouse dies. *"Second-to-die" life insurance* can work in that situation.

    However, when the beneficiary of a policy is not your spouse, the death benefit may be subject to federal estate taxes, as well. Buying life insurance through an *irrevocable life insurance trust* can shield the proceeds from estate taxation. See an estate-planning lawyer for more information and help with setting up this type of trust.

- **Wiping out debt.** If you plan to still be paying off your mortgage or the mortgage on a new retirement home or vacation property in retirement and you don't want your spouse to be burdened with that debt after you're gone, life insurance could provide enough cash for your estate to pay it off immediately. Or you may want the death benefit to be used to pay the bills for your funeral and burial.

- **Making a donation.** If a charity is named both owner and beneficiary of a policy on your life and it's an irrevocable gift, you get a tax deduction equal to the value of the policy at the time you make the gift (usually that's a little more than the cash-surrender value or the replacement value).

What You Might Drop

If the analysis of your life insurance shows that you've got more insurance than you need, drop your term policies first. The premiums on these policies are generally very high later in life, so they're probably not worth renewing. Cash-value policies that don't pay dividends aren't worth keeping either. Hold on to paid-up cash-value policies that have good internal rates of return, especially if you don't need the money that's tied up in them. Some are earning 7% to 8.5% with annual death-benefit costs of only about 0.75%. You get the advantage of tax-free growth, and when you die no income tax is due. You could probably beat that performance by cashing out the policy and investing the money in mutual funds, but you'll be taxed on the difference between the cash value and the premiums you paid.

Consider Borrowing

To get some cash out without surrendering the policy, you can borrow against the cash value of a policy tax-free, and usually at favorable rates. You don't have to pay the money back, but your death benefit will be reduced by the amount of your outstanding loan. Don't let the amount you borrow plus interest exceed the cash value, or the policy will self-destruct and you'll owe taxes as if you had surrendered it. You can also convert an unneeded policy into current income by rolling it into an annuity—a tax-free exchange. (For more on choosing an annuity, see page 30.) If you're still paying for a policy that you don't really need, you can choose to have the face value reduced in exchange for paying no more premiums.

A Well-crafted Will

If you don't have a will, your state will, in effect, write one for you after your death, and your assets will be distributed according to state law. In some states, if a couple has no children, the death of a spouse leaves the survivor with only half of his or her estate—the other half goes to the deceased's relatives. If there is one child, the survivor and child split the total, and if there are two or more children, the survivor gets only a third.

Instead of leaving your affairs in the hands of the state, take the time to have a thorough will drafted. It will guarantee that your hard-earned assets are distributed to those you want to receive them and it could save you thousands of dollars in estate taxes. In addition, a will ensures that your estate will be administered by whomever you name as executor and not by someone appointed by the court.

The federal estate-tax laws permit you pass on to heirs up to $600,000 (plus an unlimited amount to your spouse) without paying any estate tax, although some state inheritance or estate taxes kick in at lower levels. Don't assume you're in the clear until you've totaled up all your assets including your house, retirement accounts, the proceeds from your life insurance, etc. Even if everything will pass to your spouse tax-free at your death, the estate-tax bill could be devastating after your spouse passes away, leaving much less for your children and grandchildren.

A will can be used to create trusts to protect some of your assets from estate taxation. Other types of trusts can be added to accomplish whatever you might want to do with your assets—pay for your grandchild's college education, make a significant gift to charity or provide both for your current spouse and your children from a previous marriage.

To do this right, you need to work with a lawyer who specializes in estate planning and will writing. And once you've written a will, go back and check it every few years to make sure it reflects your current wishes. It may also need updating due to changes in federal or state law. Here are some key questions your will should address:

- ***How will the proceeds of the estate be distributed?*** This should include all your major assets. You might want to add a personal letter that describes how you want your personal belongings distributed so your heirs won't squabble over who should get your golf clubs, your grandmoth-

er's pearls or your wedding china.
- ***Who will be the executor?*** Who will make sure that the provisions of your will are carried out? This should be someone you trust, but also someone who has the organizational and diplomatic skills necessary for the job.
- ***If you have minor children, who will take care of them?*** Your will should appoint a guardian, and if you're leaving assets to minors, your will should state at what age they are to receive their inheritance. Or you may also want to create a trust that provides for the management and distribution of those assets.

Significant life changes, such as marriage, divorce or moving to a new state, usually require that your will be rewritten for it to comply with state laws. If you move to a distant state, you may want to change your executor—and maybe even your children's guardian—to someone who is close by.

Finally, beware of do-it-yourself wills. If not properly signed and witnessed in accordance with state law, they may be invalid. Your estate will then be treated as if there were no will at all.

Other Important Pieces of Your Plan

In addition to a will, some other documents are vital to creating an estate plan that will work. The following are some of the most important:

A Personal Inventory

In order for your executor and your survivors to take care of your affairs after your death, they need to know what you own and where all your important papers are kept. A personal inventory should include basic information about you, your spouse and your children (birth dates, social security numbers and addresses and phone numbers), as well as addresses and phone numbers for your lawyer, accountant, primary bank, broker, financial planner, insurance agent and any other professionals you use, including the manager of your pension plan.

It should also list all your assets and note where you keep important documents such as your will, insurance policies, stock certificates, investment records and birth certificate. Give a copy of this inventory to your lawyer and executor and make sure your spouse and a few other trusted relatives or friends know where it is kept.

Durable Power of Attorney

A power of attorney document authorizes another person to act on your behalf, and a *durable* power of attorney continues to be effective even when you become incapacitated or incompetent. The person to which you give the power—known as the agent or the attorney-in-fact—can then use your assets to care for you and your family should you become unable to do so due to an accident, illness or injury. The power of attorney document can specify exactly what powers you want your agent to have and it can even instruct that person as to *how* you would want him or her to use your resources on your behalf.

Advanced Directive

This is a document that lets you have a say in what kind of medical care you should receive if you are seriously ill or injured and unable to speak for yourself. The two types of advanced directives are living wills and health care powers of attorney.

- ***A living will*** is basically a statement of your wishes about what kind of care you would want if you were in a coma as a result of an auto accident, for example, or in some other situation where your family might not be sure whether you would want a doctor to take steps to keep you alive. But because there have been cases of medical professionals or even family members ignoring the wishes expressed in such documents, many experts recommend health-care powers of attorney instead of or in addition to a living will.
- ***A health-care power of attorney*** lets you name an agent to make decisions for you about your health care. In the power of attorney document, you can also provide your agent with guidelines and instructions about the extent of

the medical care you would want under various circumstances and what quality of life is acceptable to you.

Depending on the nature of your assets and the needs of your survivors, other legal tools may need to be included in your estate plan. For example, if you own a small business, you may want to draw up a separate document that outlines the steps you want taken either to dissolve your business or pass it on to the next generation. Or if you have a child who is disabled or has special needs and relies on your care, you'll want to develop a trust and make other arrangements to make sure that person will be cared for after you're gone.

Conclusion

Having worked your way through this guidebook, you've already taken an important first step in building your personal plan for a successful retirement. Armed with the information you've acquired, you're now ready to take action. And as we established early on, the sooner you start, the better off you'll be.

In the introduction to this book, we suggested you decide now when you want to retire. After examining your financial situation in Part 2, you may have decided you can afford to retire sooner than you thought or that you'd be better off waiting a few more years. You may even have decided that you never want to "retire" in the traditional sense of the word—that you want to keep working in your field as long as you can or that there are other career avenues you want to explore.

No matter what goal you've decided to shoot for, now's the time to start taking action. That doesn't mean you need to sit down and work out everything we've covered in this guidebook, but you should set short-, medium- and long-term goals for yourself now, while all this is fresh in your mind.

Break up the process of creating your retirement plan into small, manageable tasks and write them down so you can keep track of how you're doing. For example, commit yourself to creating an inventory of all your assets, including finding and organizing related documents, over the next six months so that you'll be ready to work out a financial plan with an adviser. Or decide that in the next month you will meet with someone to create a plan for paying off all your debt over the next five years. After that you can start putting more money into your retirement savings.

Whatever you decide is most important to getting your planning underway, focus on what you need to do to accomplish that and get started on it now. As you meet each goal that you set for yourself, you'll be encouraged to keep going and you'll find that your idea of a successful retirement is not that far out of reach.